Instant Vortex Dual Basket Air Fryer Cookbook

Healthy and Easy Vortex Plus 2-Basket Air Fryer Recipes

By

Anna Moore

Copyright [Anna Moore]

All rights reserved. No part of this guide may be reproduced in any form without permission in writing from the publisher except in the case of brief quotations embodied in critical articles or reviews.

Table of Contents

Introduction 7
Why Use a 2-Basket Air Fryer Cookbook? 8
How To Use This Model? 9
Smart Programs 13
Breakfast 16
    Apple Fritters 16
    Breakfast Potatoes 16
    Air Fryer Granola 17
    Banana Bread 17
    Sweet Potato Hash 18
    Monkey Bread 18
    Sausage Patties 19
    Breakfast Egg Rolls 19
    Baked Apples 20
    French Toast Sticks 20
Lunch 21
    Baked Potatoes 21
    Roasted Vegetables 21
    Cacio e Pepe Spaghetti Squash 22
    Acorn Squash with Black Beans, Corn, and Cheese 22
    Roasted Butternut Squash and kale Salad with Balsamic-Maple Dressing ... 23
    Hash Browns 23
    Corn On The Cob 24
    Falafel 24
    Roasted Potatoes 25
    Roasted Mushrooms 25
Appetizers and Side Dishes 26
    Sweet Potato Fries 26
    Garlic Parmesan Carrot Fries 26
    Grilled Dumplings 27
    Sweet Potato Tots 27
    Italian Stuffed Tomatoes 28
    Sweet Carrots 28

Garlic Fries With Rosemary 29

Roasted Cauliflower 29

Roasted Pineapple 30

Roasted Brussels Sprouts with Maple-Mustard Mayo 30

Fish & Seafood 31

Mahi Mahi 31

COD 31

Tilapia 32

Swordfish 32

Haddock 33

Roasted Salmon 33

Baked Crab Cakes 34

Roasted Fish Sticks 34

Grilled Blackened Tilapia 35

Grilled Mahi Mahi Tacos 35

Poultry 36

Bone-In Chicken Breast 36

Whole Chicken 36

Orange Chicken 37

Fried Chicken 37

Stuffed Chicken Breast 38

Cornish Hen 38

Lemon Pepper Wings 39

Grilled Chicken 39

Shake & Bake Chicken 40

Pineapple Chicken 40

Chicken Tenders 41

Ranch Chicken 41

Turkey Breast Roast 42

Chicken Skewers 42

Chicken Nuggets 43

Sesame Chicken Thighs 43

Chicken Calzone 44

Chicken Cutlet 44

Chicken Taco Pockets 45

Chicken Meatballs 45

Meat 46

Pork Belly Bites 46

Pork Roast 46

Pork Chops 47

Lamb Roast 47

Lamb Chops 48

Country Style Ribs 48

Beef Roast 49

Beef Tips 49

Steak Wrapped Asparagus 50

Cheeseburger Pockets 50

Nachos 51

Taco Pie 51

Beef and Bean Taquitos 52

Meatballs 52

Beef & Bean Chimichangas 53

Manwich Sloppy Joe Bombs 53

Pizza Burgers 54

Taco Pizza 54

Spiral Ham 55

Bacon-Wrapped Hot Dogs 55

Vegetables 56

Stuffed Sweet Potatoes 56

Garlic-Herb Fried Patty Pan Squash 56

Beets with Orange Gremolata and Goat Cheese 57

Bacon Wrapped Avocado Wedges 57

Roasted Green Beans 58

Mushroom Roll-Ups 58

Eggplant Parm 59

Eggplant Fries 59

Broccoli & Cauliflower 60

Bok Choy 60

Desserts 61
   Air Fried Oreos 61
   S'MORES 61
   Cookies 62
   Lava Cake 62
   Peach Cobbler 63
   Cinnamon Sugar Dessert Fries 63
   Pumpkin Pie Twists 64
   Brownies 64
   Apple Hand Pies 65
   Bread Pudding 65
Conclusion 66
Conversion Charts 67
Notes 69

Introduction

Welcome to the *Vortex Dual Basket Air Fryer Oven Cookbook*. Finding the time to make scrumptious, healthful meals in today's hectic environment can be difficult. This cookbook is your key to utilizing the Vortex Dual Basket Air Fryer Oven's full potential as a tool for effective and pleasurable cooking.

The Vortex Dual Basket Air Fryer Oven is an indispensable piece of kitchen equipment that provides a healthier alternative to conventional cooking techniques without sacrificing flavor. The distinctive dual-basket design of this air fryer oven makes it stand out since it enables you to cook multiple items at once while consuming less time and energy.

This cookbook is necessary to get the best out of your Vortex Dual Basket Air Fryer Oven. Whether you are a busy professional or a budding home cook, this cookbook meets your culinary goals. It provides a variety of recipes that you can use with your air fryer oven to fry, bake, roast, grill, and even dehydrate foods, ranging from mouth-watering breakfast fare to decadent sweets. Before you start your culinary adventure, we'll provide thorough instructions on using your Vortex Dual Basket Air Fryer Oven. You'll develop a thorough understanding of its features, settings, and operations, enabling you to maximize its performance and create culinary marvels easily.

Get ready to set out on a tasty and practical cooking adventure. Make cooking enjoyable, effective, and tasty by making the *Vortex Dual Basket Air Fryer Oven Cookbook* your go-to kitchen partner. Have fun cooking!

Why Use a 2-Basket Air Fryer Cookbook?

A 2-basket air fryer cookbook can be useful for owners of the Vortex Air Fryer Dual Basket Oven in several ways. Some of the advantages are as follows:

Variety Of Recipes:

The Vortex Air Fryer Dual Basket Oven Cookbook provides many recipes. You can use your air fryer to make various foods, including appetizers, entrées, sides, and desserts.

Efficient Cooking:

You can make several things simultaneously with two baskets, saving time and energy. It is especially helpful when cooking for a family or many guests.

Healthy Cooking:

Air frying is a healthy cooking method that uses little or no oil. This cookbook is designed for 2-basket air fryers, including recipes focusing on healthy cooking methods.

Less Mess:

Air frying has much less mess and less cleanup than conventional frying techniques. You can follow the instructions in this cookbook to use the two baskets effectively and cut down on cleanup.

Temperature And Time Guidance:

This cookbook includes detailed directions for cooking times and temperatures for all the recipes. Your meals will always be prepared to perfection, thanks to this.

Beginner-Friendly:

This beginner-friendly cookbook offers comprehensive, step-by-step directions. This will make it simpler for people new to air frying to get going and cook delectable meals.

Time-Saving:

Air fryers generally cook food faster than traditional ways, and this cookbook can help you maximize this time-saving benefit.

Reduced Odors:

Compared to conventional frying, air frying produces fewer culinary odors, which can help keep the kitchen smelling clean.

How To Use This Model?

The Instant Vortex Plus Dual Air Fryer is a multifunctional kitchen appliance made to improve the convenience and health of cooking. You may prepare multiple foods using two separate baskets, saving time and effort. Thanks to quick air circulation technology, it crisps and cooks food with little to no oil, giving it the ideal crispy texture while lowering bad fats. It offers many smart cooking options to fit your culinary preferences, including Air Fry, Roast, Bake, Grill, Dehydrate, and Reheat. Thanks to the user-friendly control panel, you can sync the baskets to finish cooking simultaneously and alter time and temperature settings. The Instant Vortex Plus Dual Air Fryer makes it easy to prepare anything, from a fast snack to a complete meal and is a useful addition to any kitchen.

Parts Of Instant Vortex Plus Dual Air Fryer

The Instant Vortex Plus Dual Air Fryer makes cooking simple and effective thanks to several essential components and add-ons. Here is a thorough breakdown of its parts:

Dual Baskets:

The air fryer has two distinct cooking chambers, each with a detachable frying basket. These baskets make the simultaneous cooking of two separate foods possible, streamlining the dinner preparation process.

Cooking Trays:

The food you're cooking is held on these perforated trays, which fit inside the cooking chambers. They let the food be cooked and crisped evenly, allowing hot air to circulate.

Control Panel:

Using the intuitive control panel, you can choose cooking programs, modify cooking time and temperature, and start or stop cooking sessions.

Power Cord:

The air fryer receives electricity from the power cord. It features a typical plug that you plug into an electrical socket.

Air Vents:

These vents at the back of the device let hot air leave while cooking, guaranteeing proper airflow and preventing overheating.

Heating Elements:

Heating elements that provide the hot air required for cooking and crisping your food are located inside the cooking chambers.

Lights:

Typically, LED lights are used to illuminate the interior of the cooking chambers, allowing you to keep an eye on the cooking process without having to open the air fryer.

Control Panel Functions

The Instant Vortex Plus Dual Air Fryer's control panel is simple to use and intuitively designed, enabling you to choose cooking programs, modify cooking parameters, and keep track of your cooking status. Here is a thorough user manual for its control panel:

Basket Selectors:

You can choose which basket you want to control by pressing one of these buttons. A "1" or "2" key press chooses the left basket and vice versa. When you wish to establish various cooking programs or parameters for each basket, use these buttons.

Smart Programs:

Typically, the control panel has buttons for various cooking options, including Air Fry, Roast, Bake, Grill, Dehydrate, and Reheat. Each of these buttons, when pressed, chooses the corresponding cooking program. These programs have predetermined temperature and time settings tailored to particular food categories.

Temperature Control:

The cooking temperature can be changed using the Temperature Control button. The display will indicate the current temperature setting when you press this button. As necessary, adjust the temperature using the Control Dial.

Time Control:

The cooking time can be modified using the Time Control button. The display will reveal the current time setting when you press this button. To adjust the cooking time as needed, turn the Control Dial.

Sync Finish:

The cooking times of both baskets are coordinated using the SyncFinish button. When turned on, it guarantees that both baskets will be done cooking simultaneously. This is especially helpful if you're cooking recipes requiring various cooking times.

SyncCook:

You can synchronize the cooking parameters, such as time and temperature, between the two baskets by pressing the SyncCook button. This is useful when you want both baskets to cook using the same program and parameters.

Start:

To start cooking using the chosen settings, click the Start button. When activated, the air fryer will begin preheating (if necessary) before cooking.

Cancel:

You can halt cooking at any time by pressing the Cancel button. Press this button to alter the settings or to end the cooking process early.

Control Dial:

You can change the time and temperature settings with the Control Dial. Use the Control Dial to raise or lower the settings when you push the Temperature or Time Control buttons. To validate your changes, turn on the Control Dial.

Sound On/Off:

You can turn on or off notification noises by holding down the Time and Temperature buttons simultaneously for 5 seconds. You may cook silently with this option since there are no sound alerts.

How To Cook?

Prep:

- Following your recipe, defrost, chop, season, or batter your ingredients.

Preheat:

- Place the air fryer's cooking basket inside.
- To cook in the left or right basket, press 1 or 2, respectively.
- The default time and temperature are displayed, and the Air Fry button blinks.
- Press the button for the smart program you wish to use to choose something other than Air Fry.
- For that smart program, the standard time and temperature are shown. Press Time and use the Control Dial to raise or reduce the cooking time as needed.
- Press Temp and use the Control Dial to raise or lower the cooking temperature if necessary.
- To start, click Start. Preheating is displayed in the status bar.
- The cooker's display changes to Add Food when it reaches the desired temperature.

Cook:

- Place your meal inside the cooking basket after removing it.
- Place the air fryer's cooking basket inside.
- The cooking countdown timer starts as soon as cooking gets going.

Turn:

- The display indicates Turn Food when the cooking cycle is halfway completed.
- After Turn Food shows, cooking will begin if the basket is not removed within 10 seconds.
- Take the basket out, then slowly rotate, flip, or turn your food.
- Reposition the basket. Cooking keeps going.

Finish:

- The air fryer beeps when the smart program is finished and the End is displayed.

Changing Cooking Time During Cooking

Smart programming can be altered once it has begun cooking:

- To choose the basket you wish to switch to, press 1 or 2.
- To increase or decrease the time, press Time and turn the Control Dial.
- To confirm the adjustment, push the Control Dial.
- To carry on cooking, click Start.

*If you don't click Start, the previous settings are used to continue cooking.

Changing Cooking Temperature During Cooking:

After starting a smart program, you can adjust the cooking temperature:

- To choose the basket you wish to switch to, press 1 or 2.
- Press Temperature, then change the Control Dial to change it.
- To confirm the adjustment, push the Control Dial.
- To carry on cooking, click Start.

Cancel Cooking During Cooking:

After beginning a smart program, you can stop cooking at any time:

- To choose the basket you want to cancel, press 1 or 2.
- Click "Cancel".

Smart Programs

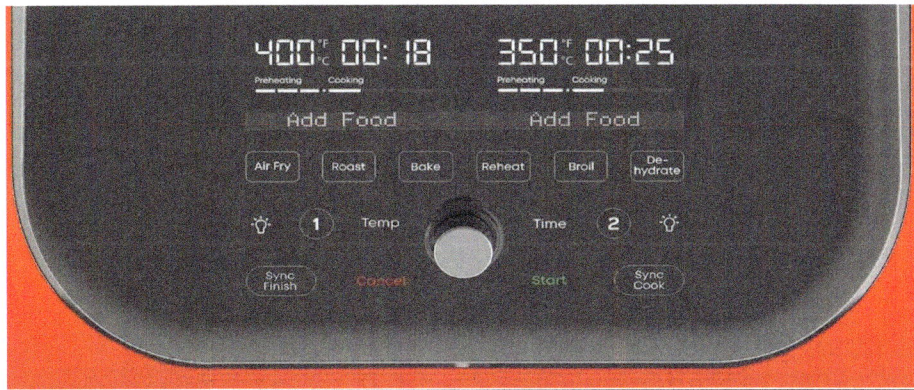

Air Fry:

You can easily air-fry foods like wings, fries, nuggets, and more.

- As necessary, defrost, chop, season, or batter your ingredients.
- Insert the cooking Basket, then select Basket 1 or 2. Select "Air Fry" from the menu. Use the Time and Temperature settings to modify the cooking time and temperature as needed.
- Select "Start" from the menu. The air fryer will start to heat up. Put your food in the basket when it says "Add Food," then push it back in.
- When instructed to "Turn Food," stop cooking and carefully turn or flip your food. Re-insert the basket to resume cooking.
- The air fryer will beep and show "End" when frying is finished. Your air-fried food will be crispy; carefully remove it and serve.

Roast:

- Prepare your roasting ingredients.
- Insert the cooking basket and choose between Basket 1 or Basket 2. Select "Roast" from the Smart Program. If required, alter the temperature and cooking time.
- To start roasting, click "Start". As it heats up, the air fryer will say, "Add Food."
- Pause cooking if instructed to spin or rotate your food for even roasting. Re-insert the basket to resume cooking.
- The air fryer will beep and show "End" when the roasting cycle ends. Take care when removing your food from the oven.

Bake:

- Get your dough or batter ready for baking.
- Insert the cooking basket and choose between Basket 1 and Basket 2. Select "Bake" from the Smart Program. If necessary, alter the temperature and cooking time.
- To start baking, click "Start". As it heats up, the air fryer will say, "Add Food."
- When the baking cycle is finished, the air fryer will beep and show "End." Take care when removing your recently baked items.

Grill:

- Prepare your grilling ingredients.
- Insert the cooking basket and choose between Basket 1 or Basket 2. Select "Grill" from the Smart Program. If necessary, adjust the cooking temperature and time.
- Grilling will begin when you press "Start". As it heats up, the air fryer will say, "Add Food."
- The air fryer will beep and show "End" when the grilling is finished. Grab your beautifully cooked creation.

Dehydrate:

- Prepare fruits and vegetables for dehydration by slicing them.
- Insert the cooking basket and choose between Basket 1 and Basket 2. Select "Dehydrate" from the Smart Program. If necessary, alter the temperature and cooking time.
- To start dehydrating, click "Start." As it heats up, the air fryer will say, "Add Food."
- The air fryer will beep and show "End" when the dehydration cycle is over. Remove your dehydrated snacks with care.

Reheat:

- In the frying basket, put your leftovers.
- Insert the cooking basket and choose between Basket 1 and Basket 2. Select "Reheat" from the Smart Program.
- To start reheating, press "Start". No need to preheat; it will begin right away.
- The air fryer will beep and show "End" when reheating is finished. Savour the warm and crispy remnants.

Using Both the Baskets

You have three choices for simultaneously cooking in both baskets when using the Vortex Dual Air Fryer:

Cook in both Baskets:

Cook simultaneously in both baskets while utilizing various settings and programs.

Sync Cook:

Using the same programming and settings for both, cook simultaneously in both baskets.

Sync Finish:

Cook simultaneously in both baskets using various settings and programs, but both cook simultaneously.

How To Cook In Both The Baskets:

- Follow the steps mentioned above for cooking, taking into account any specific instructions for the smart program you wish to utilize:
- Initiate the configuration of your initial program within the left basket by selecting "1." You can make adjustments to the time and temperature settings if desired.
- To establish a second smart program within the right basket, press "2." Be sure to customize the time and temperature settings as needed.
- Finally, press the "Start" button and follow the cooking instructions provided.

How To Sync Cook:

- Please follow the cooking guidelines mentioned above, considering any specific instructions about the smart program you intend to employ.
- Once you've configured your initial program (in either basket), but before initiating the cooking process by pressing the Start button, activate the SyncCook feature.
- You will notice the SyncCook icon displayed. Subsequently, press the Start button and follow the provided cooking instructions.

How To Sync Finish:

- Follow the cooking instructions above and any specific directions for your preferred smart program.
- Configure your initial program in either basket, selecting either 1 or 2, and feel free to adjust the time and temperature settings according to your preferences.
- Subsequently, select the opposite basket by pressing 1 or 2 and begin configuring a smart program for that basket, making any necessary modifications to the time and temperature settings.

Breakfast

Apple Fritters

Cooking Time: 10 min | Serves: 12 | Per Serving: Calories 221, Carbs 46g, Fat 3g, Protein 3g.

Ingredients:
- 1/3 tsp ground nutmeg
- 1 tbsp baking powder
- 2 eggs
- ½ cup granulated sugar
- ¼ tsp ground cloves
- 2 large apples
- 3 tbsp melted butter
- 1 tsp cinnamon
- 2 cups all-purpose flour
- 1 tsp vanilla
- ¾ cup apple juice/apple cider
- 1 tsp salt

Apple Cider Glaze
- ¼ tsp nutmeg
- 2 cups powdered sugar
- ½ tsp cinnamon
- 1/4 cup apple juice/apple cider

Directions:
Peel and core the apples. Cut into pieces of a quarter of an inch. Spread the apple chunks out on a kitchen towel to remove the moisture. Mix the flour, sugar, salt, baking powder, and spices in a bowl. Mix the flour with the apples. Whisk together the eggs, butter, vanilla, and apple cider in a small bowl. The flour mixture and the wet mixture are combined. Set the air fryer's temperature to 390°F. Put some silicone mat or parchment paper in the bottom of the air fryer basket. Take an ice cream scooper to place three to four dollops of fritter dough in the air fryer. Spray the oil on the fritters' top. For six minutes, cook. Turn over and cook for a further four minutes.

Breakfast Potatoes

Cooking Time: 10 min | Serves: 02 | Per Serving: Calories 375, Carbs 67g, Fat 7g, Protein 13g.

Ingredients:
- ½ tsp garlic powder
- 1 tbsp oil
- ¼ tsp ground black pepper
- ½ tsp kosher salt
- 5 peeled and cubed potatoes
- ½ tsp smoked paprika

Directions:
The air fryer should be preheated at 400F for two to three minutes. This gives the crispiest potatoes. In the meantime, generously coat the potatoes with oil and morning potato spice. Spray some nonstick cooking spray on the air fryer basket. To ensure consistent cooking, stop cooking after adding the potatoes and shake the basket a couple of times during the next fifteen minutes. Serve immediately after transferring to a plate.

Air Fryer Granola

Cooking Time: 15 min | Serves: 08 | Per Serving: Calories 336, Carbs 38g, Fat 19g, Protein 7g.

Ingredients:
- 1/8 cup chopped hazelnuts
- 1 tbsp flax seed
- 1/8 cup pepitas
- 2 tbsp honey
- 1/8 cup chopped almonds
- 6 tbsp olive oil
- 1/8 cup chopped walnuts
- ½ tsp vanilla extract
- 1/8 tsp ground cloves
- ¼ cup dried blueberries
- 1/8 cup chopped pecans
- ½ tsp ground cinnamon
- ¼ cup maple syrup
- 2 cup rolled oats
- ¼ cup dried cherries
- 1/8 tsp ground cloves
- ¼ cup maple syrup
- 1/8 cup dried cranberries
- ½ cup toasted wheat germ

Directions:
In a bowl, combine each dry ingredient. Combine the oil, maple syrup, and honey or agave in a bowl. The dry ingredients should be thoroughly coated as you combine the syrup. Heat the air fryer to 350 degrees. The granola should be golden brown after fifteen minutes of baking at 350 degrees, stirring every five mins. Store in an airtight jar, allow to cool, and keep for up to three weeks.

Banana Bread

Cooking Time: 20 min | Serves: 06 | Per Serving: Calories 240, Carbs 39g, Fat 14g, Protein 3g.

Ingredients:
- 1 tsp baking soda
- ½ cup oil
- 1 tsp salt
- 3 overripe bananas
- ½ cup milk
- 1 tsp cinnamon
- 2/3 cup sugar
- 1 tsp baking powder
- 1 1/3 cups flour

Directions:
In a mixer or a mixing bowl, combine each item. After that, use olive oil or non-stick cooking spray to coat your pan. Bake in the air fryer for twenty to thirty minutes at 330 degrees Fahrenheit. If a toothpick is inserted into the banana bread, is it clean? If so, it is done; if not, give it a few more minutes. Slice after cooling, then plate.

Sweet Potato Hash

Cooking Time: 20 min | Serves: 04 | Per Serving: Calories 199, Carbs 20g, Fat 11g, Protein 5g.

Ingredients:
- ¼ tsp kosher salt
- 2 sweet potatoes cut into cubes
- ¼ tsp ground black pepper
- 4 strips bacon (diced)
- ½ cup yellow diced onion
- 2 tbsp dark brown sugar
- 1 tsp dried rosemary
- 2 tbsp olive oil

Directions:
Set the air fryer to 400°F. Brown sugar and diced bacon should be combined in a small basin, coated, and put aside. Sweet potatoes, onion, rosemary, olive oil, salt, and pepper should all be mixed in a mixing bowl. Stir till the potatoes are thoroughly coated. The mixture should be added to an air fryer that has been preheated. Open the basket, stir the mixture, then top the hash with the bacon coated in brown sugar. Back in the air fryer, cook for six more minutes. Stir once more, then simmer for an additional six to seven minutes, till the potatoes are soft inside and faintly crispy on the outside, & the bacon is crisp and fully cooked.

Monkey Bread

Cooking Time: 20 min | Serves: 06 | Per Serving: Calories 2411, Carbs 452g, Fat 27g, Protein 53g.

Ingredients:
- ½ cup brown sugar
- 4 tbsp melted butter
- 1 tsp cinnamon
- 12 white dinner rolls

Glaze
- ½ tsp vanilla
- 2 tbsp milk
- ½ cup powdered sugar

Directions:
Combine cinnamon and brown sugar in a small bowl. Melt a quarter stick of butter in a separate bowl. Melted butter should be lightly brushed inside of an air fryer-compatible oven-safe pan. Rolls should be split in half, rolled in butter, then dunked in the sugar mixture before being placed in the pan once they have thawed to room temperature. Repeat! Place all the rolls in the pan and sprinkle with the remaining butter and sugar. Rolls should rise in an air fryer that has been warmed and turned OFF for 30 minutes. Rolls should be carefully covered with foil to avoid the top from burning before baking for ten to twenty minutes at 340 °F. It is cooked when a bread instant-read thermometer registers around 180 °F. While baking, prepare the glaze by mixing milk, vanilla, and powdered sugar till it is barely runny. Remove the foil to slightly brown the top and bake for one to three more minutes. With oven mitts, carefully remove the pan from the oven. Just one minute of cooling is all that is needed before flipping the pan over onto a dish. Glaze it, then indulge.

Sausage Patties

Cooking Time: 06 min | Serves: 04 | Per Serving: Calories 140, Carbs 10g, Fat 3g, Protein 12g.

Ingredients:
- 8 raw sausage patties

Directions:
Heat the air fryer to 350°F. Add the frozen sausage patties to the air fryer and cook for four to five minutes or until well warmed.

Breakfast Egg Rolls

Cooking Time: 10 min | Serves: 04 | Per Serving: Calories 258, Carbs 8g, Fat 19g, Protein 13g.

Ingredients:
- ½ cup shredded cheddar cheese
- 4 egg roll wrappers
- Pinch of salt
- 1 tsp butter
- 4 cooked & crumbled slices of bacon
- Pinch of pepper
- 4 eggs

Directions:
To prepare these delectable egg rolls, preheat your cooking method based on your preference: a deep fryer to 350°F, an oven to 425°F, or an air fryer to 390°F. Now, crack the eggs into a small bowl, season them with a pinch of salt and pepper, and whisk them together until well blended. In a medium frying pan, melt the butter over medium heat. Sprinkle the cheddar cheese and crumbled bacon on top of the eggs, and stir everything together until the eggs are fully cooked. Lay an egg roll wrapper flat with one of its points facing you. Use a brush to moisten the edges with water. Place approximately a quarter of the egg mixture in the center of the wrapper. Fold in the left and right corners, then fold the bottom corner. Roll the egg roll away from you and seal the top point with additional water, if necessary. Repeat this process with the remaining three wrappers. For air frying, arrange the egg rolls in the basket, ensuring they don't touch, and lightly brush them with olive oil. Air fry for about 8 mins, flipping them halfway through cooking. These homemade egg rolls will surely delight your taste buds no matter your chosen cooking method. Enjoy!

Baked Apples

Cooking Time: 15 min | Serves: 02 | Per Serving: Calories 350, Carbs 57g, Fat 14g, Protein 4g.

Ingredients:
- 2 tbsp all-purpose flour
- ¾ tsp ground cinnamon
- 2 tbsp pecans
- ½ cup rolled oats
- 2 tbsp brown sugar
- Pinch of salt
- 2 medium apples
- 2 tbsp unsalted butter

Directions:
Some toppings may bubble over, so get air fryer ready as necessary. Use parchment paper in the air fryer, but that approach might not suit many models. Set the air fryer's temperature to 325 °F. Combine the ingredients aside from the apples and raisins in a small mixing dish. Each apple should have a spoonful of raisins in the center. You should place the raisins between the apples and the crumble to prevent burning. To prevent the crumble topping from moving around in the air fryer, divide it among the four apple halves and press it firmly over the raisins. The crumble topping side should face up as you gently drop them in the air fryer. Bake for thirteen to eighteen minutes until softened. The crumble mixture will begin to brown, and the apples will have softened but not become mushy. As they sit, they'll soften a little bit more.

French Toast Sticks

Cooking Time: 32 min | Serves: 04 | Per Serving: Calories 323, Carbs 56g, Fat 6g, Protein 11g.

Ingredients:
- 2 tbsp milk
- Cooking spray
- ¼ tsp ground cinnamon (divided)
- 4 eggs
- ½ cup granulated sugar
- 6 slices of white bread
- ½ tsp vanilla extract

Directions:
Spray cooking spray liberally all over the air fryer basket. At 350 degrees F, let the air fryer heat for about five minutes. Cut each slice of bread in half vertically, then in half horizontally, creating four sticks. Combine the eggs, milk, vanilla essence, and one-fourth tsp cinnamon in a medium bowl. Whisk until everything is thoroughly combined. To make the cinnamon-sugar mixture, combine sugar and the last tsp of cinnamon in a small bowl. Breadsticks should be thoroughly coated on both sides. Working in batches of six, dunk bread sticks into the egg mixture. Sticks should be placed in the air fryer with room between them after being sprinkled with the cinnamon-sugar mixture on either side. Cook for four minutes, flip it, and cook for another four minutes. Serve with whipped cream, syrup, or confectioners' sugar.

Lunch

Baked Potatoes

Cooking Time: 60 min | Serves: 04 | Per Serving: Calories 251, Carbs 49g, Fat 4g, Protein 6g.

Ingredients:
- ½ tsp ground pepper
- Light sour cream
- ¼ tsp salt
- 1 tbsp olive oil
- Chopped chives
- 8 oz. russet potatoes

Directions:
A 6-quart or bigger air fryer should be preheated for five minutes at 390°F. With a fork, prick potatoes all over (approximately sixteen times). Season the potatoes with salt and pepper after applying oil. Place the potatoes in the air fryer basket spaced about one inch apart. Cook for about fifty minutes or till the potatoes are soft to the touch, and the skins are crisp and golden. Observe for five minutes. Slice lengthwise in half. Serve with yogurt or sour cream, and top with chives.

Roasted Vegetables

Cooking Time: 10 min | Serves: 04 | Per Serving: Calories 37, Carbs 3g, Fat 2g, Protein 1g.

Ingredients:
- ½ cup diced summer squash
- ¼ tsp salt
- ½ cup diced asparagus
- ¼ tsp ground black pepper
- ½ cup diced sweet pepper
- ¼ tsp seasoning
- ½ cup diced cauliflower
- 2 tsp vegetable oil
- ½ cup diced mushrooms, zucchini and mushrooms

Directions:
Assemble all the components. Gather all the ingredients for the air fryer-roasted vegetables. Set the air fryer's temperature to 360°F (180°C). Fill the bowl with the following ingredients: cauliflower, oil, zucchini, mushrooms, asparagus, pepper, red pepper, squash, salt, and any additional seasonings. Place in the frying basket in a single layer after tossing to coat.

Cacio e Pepe Spaghetti Squash

Cooking Time: 40 min | Serves: 02 | Per Serving: Calories 258, Carbs 18g, Fat 18g, Protein 6g.

Ingredients:
- 2 tbsp olive oil
- ½ tsp black pepper
- 2 lb. spaghetti squash
- ¾ tsp kosher salt
- 2 tbsp grated Parmesan
- Torn basil leaves

Directions:
The spaghetti squash should be split lengthwise. The center of each half should be scooped out, and any stringy pieces should be discarded. Sprinkle black pepper & salt over the cut sides of the spaghetti squash halves and drizzle them with olive oil. Over the squash halves, equally distribute the grated Parmesan. Set your air fryer to bake mode, normally at a temperature of 375°F (190°C). Put the cut-side-up spaghetti squash halves on the air frying rack or in the air fryer basket. Bake the squash for thirty to forty minutes or till it is soft and easily punctured with a fork. Depending on your air fryer model, cooking times may vary, so check the squash frequently. Squash flesh can be made into "spaghetti" using a fork to scrape it into strands. Serve the spaghetti squash on plates after it has been shredded. Add more olive oil, extra grated Parmesan cheese to taste, and freshly ground black pepper. To enhance taste and freshness, garnish with torn basil leaves.

Acorn Squash with Black Beans, Corn, and Cheese

Cooking Time: 20 min | Serves: 03 | Per Serving: Calories 392, Carbs 34g, Fat 15g, Protein 13g.

Ingredients:
- ¼ tsp + 1/8 tsp kosher salt
- ½ cup cooked black beans
- ¼ tsp sweet paprika
- 1 lb. acorn squash halved
- ½ tsp chili powder
- 1 cup shredded cheddar cheese
- ¼ tsp ground cumin
- Olive oil cooking spray
- 1 seeded & chopped tomato
- Fresh cilantro leaves

Directions:
Slice the acorn squash in half, then remove the seeds and stringy parts. Add freshly ground black pepper and one-eighth tsp of kosher salt to the squash halves. Turn on the bake setting on the air fryer, usually at 375°F (190°C). Cut side facing up, place the seasoned acorn squash halves in the air fryer basket or on the air fryer rack. Squash halves are lightly sprayed with a cooking spray containing olive oil. The squash should be baked for twenty to twenty-five minutes or till fork-tender and easily punctured. Make the filling and bake the squash simultaneously. The diced tomato, black beans, frozen corn, chili powder, cumin, sweet paprika, a quarter of a tsp kosher salt, and a dash of black pepper should all be combined in a basin. Mix thoroughly. Remove the acorn squash from the air fryer when it is soft-cooked. The black beans, corn, and squash mixture should go inside each half. Sprinkle half of the cheddar cheese grated over each half. The squash halves with the filling should be placed back in the air fryer and baked for five to seven minutes or till the cheese is bubbling and melted. Before serving, scatter some fresh cilantro leaves over the packed acorn squash. Serve the acorn squash with the corn, black beans, and cheese immediately after cooking while the food is hot.

Roasted Butternut Squash and kale Salad with Balsamic-Maple Dressing

Cooking Time: 20 min | Serves: 04 | Per Serving: Calories 227, Carbs 19g, Fat 10g, Protein 4g.

Ingredients:
- 2 tsp balsamic vinegar
- ¼ cup dried cranberries
- 2 oz. goat cheese
- 1 tsp Dijon mustard
- 2 tbsp + 2 tsp olive oil
- 2 lb. butternut squash cut into pieces
- ¼ tsp black pepper
- 2 tbsp raw pumpkin seeds (pepitas)
- 1 tsp kosher salt
- 1 bunch of curly kale
- 2 tsp maple syrup

Directions:
Mix the squash in a big bowl with two tsp of oil, half tsp of salt, and one-fourth tsp of pepper. Reserve the bowl and scrape into an air fryer basket. Cook for fifteen mins at 400°, shaking the basket or tossing the squash occasionally, till it is soft and golden. Meanwhile, combine the remaining two tbsp. oil, vinegar, syrup, mustard, and half tsp salt in the bowl you set aside. Add the greens and stir the dressing to soften it slightly. Add the squash and greens to a bowl. Season with pepper and salt and mix in the cranberries and pepitas. Add goat cheese crumbles to the salad and stir gently.

Hash Browns

Cooking Time: 25 min | Serves: 04 | Per Serving: Calories 90, Carbs 13g, Fat 2g, Protein 2g.

Ingredients:
- 1 tbsp vegetable oil
- 3 cup peeled & grated potatoes
- ¾ tsp salt
- ¼ cup water

Directions:
Toss the potatoes with the water in a medium basin till they are completely covered. Wrap in plastic wrap and make several fork slits in the plastic. After placing the mixture in the microwave, cook it for three and a half to four minutes, stirring the mixture every minute or till the potatoes are almost tender but still have some bite. Let the potatoes cool before tossing them with salt and oil. Form the hash browns into six 1" thick, rectangular pucks after they are ready to be handled. Heat the air fryer to 400 degrees, then cook the hash browns for fifteen to twenty minutes or till they are crispy and golden brown.

Corn On The Cob

Cooking Time: 20 min | Serves: 04 | Per Serving: Calories 258, Carbs 29g, Fat 11g, Protein 12g.

Ingredients:
- 3 tbsp chopped red onion
- ½ tsp smoked or sweet paprika
- 1 cup crumbled feta
- 1 ¼ tsp dried oregano
- Lemon wedges
- 4 ears of corn
- 2 tsp chopped basil
- ½ cup Full-fat Greek Yogurt

Directions:
Set the air fryer to the grill mode by preheating it to a high temperature, usually between 400 and 450 °F (200 and 230 °C). Remove all of the corn's husks and silk by shucking it. Cut the ears in half to fit into the air fryer if the ears are huge. The Greek yogurt, finely chopped red onion, dried oregano, fresh basil, and sweet or smoked paprika should all be combined in a mixing dish with the crumbled feta. Stir the ingredients to mix them thoroughly. Directly place the corn into the air fryer's preheated grill. When turning the corn every few minutes, grill it for about five to seven minutes or until it's well-roasted and cooked to the desired doneness. Transfer the air-fried corn to a serving tray after removing it from the appliance. The hot, grilled corn should be covered liberally with the feta mixture.

Falafel

Cooking Time: 35 min | Serves: 20 | Per Serving: Calories 64, Carbs 7g, Fat 3g, Protein 2g.

Ingredients:
- 1 tsp dried coriander
- ½ cup yellow onion
- 1 tsp baking powder
- 4 garlic cloves
- 1 tsp kosher salt
- 1/3 cup tahini
- 3 tbsp water
- ¼ cup packed cilantro leaves
- 2 oz. cans chickpeas
- ½ lemon juice
- 2 tsp ground cumin
- ¼ cup parsley leaves
- ½ tsp crushed red pepper flakes

Directions:
Garlic, onion, cilantro, and parsley should all be roughly diced in a food processor. Add the chickpeas, half tsp of red pepper flakes, baking powder, cumin, salt, and coriander. Stop before the mixture turns into a paste after pulsing the chickpeas till they are mostly broken down with some pieces. Adjust seasonings based on taste. Scoop around two tbsp of the chickpea mixture, gently shape it into a ball, and do not over-squeeze; otherwise, the falafel will be dense. Place the balls in an air fryer basket in batches. Cook for about fifteen mins at 370° till browned.

Meanwhile, the lemon juice and tahini should be combined in a medium bowl. Red pepper flakes and salt should be added, and the water should be added one tablespoon at a time till the appropriate consistency is achieved. Serve falafel plain or with sauce and in a pita or salad.

Roasted Potatoes

Cooking Time: 25 min | Serves: 04 | Per Serving: Calories 158, Carbs 31g, Fat 2g, Protein 3g.

Ingredients:
- 2.2 lb. Sebago potatoes
- Salt to season
- Olive oil spray

Directions:
Cut the potatoes into four cm cubes after peeling. Utilizing a fresh tea towel, dry the potatoes. Put potatoes in the air fryer's basket. Spray liberally with oil, toss, and repeat as necessary. Cook for fifteen minutes at 300 °F. Stir the basket. Cook for ten minutes or till brown and crisp, increasing heat to 350°F. Salt the potatoes before serving.

Roasted Mushrooms

Cooking Time: 10 min | Serves: 04 | Per Serving: Calories 131, Carbs 7g, Fat 11g, Protein 3g.

Ingredients:
- 1 tbsp soy sauce
- Freshly ground black pepper
- 1 lb. large fresh mushrooms
- ½ tsp garlic powder
- 3 tbsp olive oil
- Freshly grated parmesan cheese

Directions:
Wash mushrooms gently in a colander. After washing the mushrooms, place them on paper towels, cover them with more paper towels, and gently press to dry them. Each mushroom should have the stem end trimmed before being cut in half. To make the cooking sauce, combine the garlic powder, olive oil, black pepper, and soy sauce in a bowl. Place the mushroom halves in a plastic dish and add the cooking liquid. Toss the mushrooms, flipping them over so they are covered. Place mushrooms cut side down in the Air Fryer basket. As necessary, heat the air fryer to 400F/200C. Cook mushrooms for five minutes. Turn the mushrooms over so the cut side is up, and cook for 5 more minutes. Remove the basket from the air fryer. If desired, top with freshly grated Parmesan cheese and serve hot.

Appetizers and Side Dishes

Sweet Potato Fries

Cooking Time: 12 min | Serves: 02 | Per Serving: Calories 232, Carbs 46g, Fat 4g, Protein 4g.

Ingredients:
- 1/8 tsp black pepper
- ¼ tsp garlic powder
- 2 sweet potatoes (peeled)
- ¼ tsp paprika
- ½ tsp salt

Directions:
Set the air fryer's temperature to 380°F. Sweet potatoes should be peeled before being cut into uniform sticks that are one-fourth inch thick. In a bowl, combine the sweet potatoes with the garlic powder, olive oil, paprika, salt, & black pepper. Depending on the basket size, cook them in two or three batches, shaking them halfway through, for twelve minutes, or until they are crispy. Depending on the air fryer, this could differ. Serve immediately with preferred dipping sauce.

Garlic Parmesan Carrot Fries

Cooking Time: 20 min | Serves: 02 | Per Serving: Calories 120, Carbs 10g, Fat 8g, Protein 2g.

Ingredients:
- 1 tbsp olive oil
- 4 carrots
- 2 tbsp grated Parmesan
- 1 crushed garlic clove
- A pinch of black pepper
- ¼ tsp crushed red pepper

Directions:
Stir the olive oil thoroughly after adding the crushed garlic. Carrots must be cleaned and dried. Cut the tops off and then divide them in half. Next, divide each half in half to make flat surfaces. You should be able to cut three strips from the larger end and two from the smaller end. Toss the fried carrots in the garlic and olive oil mixture. Combine the black and red pepper with the Parmesan. Sprinkle the pepper and Parmesan mix over the fries covered in the oil mixture. A baking sheet or an air fryer basket should be filled with an even layer of carrot fries. For crispier carrot fries, bake at 350 for sixteen to twenty minutes while tossing the pan halfway through. Add finely chopped parsley or parsley flakes on top.

Grilled Dumplings

Cooking Time: 10 min | Serves: 05 | Per Serving: Calories 200, Carbs 20g, Fat 6g, Protein 8g.

Ingredients:
- 1 tbsp olive oil
- ½ tsp grated ginger
- Red pepper flakes
- ½ tsp sugar
- Chopped green onions
- 1 minced garlic clove
- ½ tsp sesame oil
- 1 tbsp rice vinegar
- 15 frozen dumplings
- 2 tbsp soy sauce

Directions:
Heat the air fryer to a high temperature, often around 400°F (200°C), and switch it to the grill mode. This will guarantee that the dumplings cook through while getting a crispy exterior. Apply a thin layer of vegetable oil to each side of each frozen dumpling. They will cook more crisply as a result of this. Arrange these dumplings in a single layer in the air fryer basket or on the grill rack. To ensure consistent cooking and browning, ensure they are not touching one another. The dumplings should be grilled for eight to ten minutes, flipping them halfway through. The size of the dumplings and the air fryer model will affect how long they need to cook, so keep a watch on them to ensure they don't burn. Prepare the dipping sauce as the dumplings are cooking. In a bowl, combine rice vinegar, soy sauce, sesame oil, finely minced ginger, garlic, sugar, and red pepper flakes. Taste the sauce, and modify the ingredients to your liking. Remove the dumplings from the air fryer when they are golden and crispy.

Sweet Potato Tots

Cooking Time: 12 min | Serves: 04 | Per Serving: Calories 26, Carbs 2g, Fat 6g, Protein 1g.

Ingredients:
- ½ cup breadcrumbs
- ½ tsp coriander
- Spray oil
- ½ tsp salt
- 2 cups sweet potato puree
- ½ tsp cumin

Directions:
Preheat the air fryer to 390°F/200°C. Mix all ingredients in a bowl. To make 1-tsp tots, place a cookie scoop on one or two plates. Spray the tots with spray oil and move them about to coat the bottoms with oil evenly. Place the tater tots on the air fryer basket, spacing them out carefully. It must be cooked in two to three batches. After six to seven minutes of cooking, carefully turn them over. When you turn the tots, if they feel mushy and squishy, wait a few more minutes. Cook for a further five to seven minutes or till crisp but not burnt on both sides. Serve immediately with guacamole, ketchup, or chipotle mayo.

Italian Stuffed Tomatoes

Cooking Time: 15 min | Serves: 04 | Per Serving: Calories 225, Carbs 23g, Fat 15g, Protein 9g.

Ingredients:
- 1/3 cup grated Parmesan cheese
- 2 tbsp chopped basil
- Olive oil
- ¼ cup crumbled goat cheese
- 2 minced garlic cloves
- ¼ cup Italian breadcrumbs
- 4 medium tomatoes
- 1 cup cooked brown rice
- 1 tbsp olive oil
- ¼ cup chopped walnuts

Directions:
Set the air fryer to bake mode and preheat it to about 375°F (190°C). This will guarantee that the stuffed tomatoes cook and brown evenly. The tomato tops should be removed and kept aside. Remove the pulp and seeds to leave the tomatoes with a hollow shell. Take care not to pierce the tomatoes' bottoms. Combine in a bowl, cooked brown rice, crumbled goat cheese, freshly grated Parmesan cheese, roasted chopped walnuts, one tbsp of fresh chopped basil, minced garlic, and half of the Italian-seasoned bread crumbs. The filling components should be thoroughly mixed. Olive oil should be lightly drizzled inside the tomatoes that have been hollowed out. This gives them taste and prevents sticking. The remaining breadcrumbs with Italian seasoning and one tbsp olive oil should be combined in a small bowl. The filled tomatoes should be evenly covered with this breadcrumb mixture. Put the filled tomatoes on the air fryer rack or in the basket and bake for around fifteen to twenty minutes, until the tomatoes are soft and the breadcrumb cover is golden brown. Take the stuffed tomatoes out of the air fryer with care.

Sweet Carrots

Cooking Time: 20 min | Serves: 04 | Per Serving: Calories 119, Carbs 17g, Fat 6g, Protein 1g.

Ingredients:
- 2 tbsp melted butter
- ¼ tsp salt
- 1 lb. of carrots peeled & chopped into pieces
- 2 tbsp brown sugar

Directions:
Stir the carrots to ensure they are completely coated in brown sugar, melted butter, and salt. Put carrots in a bowl that can go in the oven and fit in the air fryer. Cook for twenty to twenty-five minutes at 380 degrees Fahrenheit while stirring every 5 minutes.

Garlic Fries With Rosemary

Cooking Time: 25 min | Serves: 08 | Per Serving: Calories 357, Carbs 33g, Fat 25g, Protein 3g.

Ingredients:
- 1 tbsp minced parsley
- ¼ cup pressed garlic
- 1 tsp kosher salt
- 1/3 cup canola oil
- ½ tsp black pepper
- 28 oz. cut fries with sea salt
- 1 tbsp minced rosemary

Directions:
Set the oven's temperature to 400 °F. On a baking sheet, distribute the fries equally and bake for fifteen to twenty minutes until they are crisp, shaking once halfway through. Combine the canola oil with the garlic, rosemary, and half a tsp of kosher salt while the fries are baking. Fries should be removed from the oven and added to a big bowl with the garlic, rosemary, and oil combination. Season with the rest of the kosher salt and freshly ground pepper. Serve right away after thoroughly mixing with tongs.

Roasted Cauliflower

Cooking Time: 15 min | Serves: 06 | Per Serving: Calories 137, Carbs 4g, Fat 13g, Protein 2g.

Ingredients:
- ¼ tsp crushed red pepper
- 1 lb. cauliflower
- ½ tsp garlic powder
- Pepper & salt to taste
- 2 tbsp grated Parmesan cheese
- ½ tsp paprika
- 1/3 cup olive oil

Directions:
Cauliflower should first be chopped into tiny pieces. Mix the garlic, olive oil, paprika, Parmesan, crushed red pepper, salt, and pepper in a small bowl. Toss the mixture with the cauliflower to coat it. Set up in an air fryer basket and cook for thirteen to fifteen minutes at 390 degrees or till crispy.

Roasted Pineapple

Cooking Time: 15 min | Serves: 02 | Per Serving: Calories 341, Carbs 89g, Fat 1g, Protein g.

Ingredients:
- 1 pineapple

Directions:
Set the air fryer to 375°F (190 degrees Celsius). With parchment paper, line the air fryer basket. Using a pineapple corer or slicer, slice the pineapple into rings. Put the prepared basket's pineapple rings inside. For eight to ten minutes in the air fryer, roast the pieces. Slices should be flipped over and air-fried for a further three to five minutes.

Roasted Brussels Sprouts with Maple-Mustard Mayo

Cooking Time: 10 min | Serves: 04 | Per Serving: Calories 240, Carbs 18g, Fat 18g, Protein 4g.

Ingredients:
- ¼ tsp kosher salt
- 1/3 cup mayonnaise
- 1 tbsp olive oil
- ¼ tsp black pepper
- 1 tbsp stone ground mustard
- 1 lb. trimmed & halved brussels sprouts
- 2 tbsp maple syrup

Directions:
Set an air fryer to 400°F (200 degrees Celsius). In a bowl, stir together 1 tbsp salt, olive oil, and pepper. Then, add the Brussels sprouts and coat well. In an air fryer basket, arrange the Brussels sprouts in only one layer without crowding them; if necessary, work in batches. Cook for four minutes. Shake the basket and cook for four to six minutes or till the sprouts are tender and deep golden brown. In the meantime, combine the mustard, remaining one tbsp of maple syrup, and mayonnaise in a small bowl. Serve the sauce mixture as a dipping sauce or toss some with the sprouts.

Fish & Seafood

Mahi Mahi

Cooking Time: 12 min | Serves: 04 | Per Serving: Calories 467, Carbs 41g, Fat 11g, Protein 48g.

Ingredients:
- ½ tsp onion powder
- 2 tbsp olive oil
- ½ tsp pepper
- 1 ½ lb. Mahi Mahi fillets
- 2 tbsp olive oil
- ½ tsp pepper
- Lemon wedges
- 2 cups breadcrumbs
- 1 tsp paprika

Directions:
The air fryer should be preheated to 400 degrees. Mahi Mahi fillets should be placed on a sizable platter and basted or drizzled with olive oil. Combine the paprika, onion powder, pepper, garlic powder, panko breadcrumbs, and salt in a bowl. Place every Mahi Mahi fillet in the air fryer basket in a single layer after being coated with the panko mixture. Spray some frying oil on. The Mahi Mahi should be cooked for twelve to fifteen minutes, turning it over halfway through. After removing them from the air fryer, serve them with lemon wedges and relish!

COD

Cooking Time: 10 min | Serves: 04 | Per Serving: Calories 302, Carbs 3g, Fat 13g, Protein 42g.

Ingredients:
- 2 tbsp lemon juice
- ½ tsp salt
- 4 cod loins
- 6 minced garlic cloves
- 1 tsp dried dill
- 4 tbsp melted butter

Directions:
Set your air fryer's temperature to 370 degrees. Combine the dill, lemon juice, butter, garlic, and salt in a bowl. Add a cod loin and coat it entirely in the basin. To prevent the garlic from falling off while cooking, lightly push it into the fish. Repeat with the rest of the cod. Put all the cod loins in the air fryer in one layer but not touching. After ten minutes of cooking, carefully remove from the air fryer. Add more butter or lemon juice to the cod's garnish if desired.

Tilapia

Cooking Time: 10 min | Serves: 04 | Per Serving: Calories 287, Carbs 3g, Fat 11g, Protein 45g.

Ingredients:
- ½ tsp onion powder
- 4 tilapia fillets
- ½ tsp salt
- Lemon wedges
- ½ tsp black pepper
- 2 tbsp olive oil
- ½ tsp garlic powder
- ½ tsp paprika

Directions:
The air fryer should be preheated to 400 degrees. On a platter, arrange the tilapia fillets and sprinkle with olive oil. Combine the garlic powder, pepper, paprika, onion powder, and salt in a bowl. Place the fillets in the air fryer in one layer after evenly seasoning them. The tilapia should be cooked for ten minutes, turning the fillets over halfway through. The tilapia should be removed from the air fryer, served with lemon wedges (if preferred), and eaten immediately.

Swordfish

Cooking Time: 08 min | Serves: 02 | Per Serving: Calories 456, Carbs 5g, Fat 0g, Protein 54g.

Ingredients:
- 1 tsp lemon pepper seasoning
- Fresh parsley
- 2 swordfish steaks (2)
- Lemon wedges
- 1 tbsp olive oil

Directions:
Set the air fryer to 400°F. Swordfish steaks should be oiled and seasoned with lemon pepper seasoning on both sides, then placed in the air fryer basket. Once the internal temperature inside reaches 145° Fahrenheit, air-fry for eight to ten mins, flipping once. Add fresh parsley as a garnish and serve with lemon wedges.

Haddock

Cooking Time: 10 min | Serves: 04 | Per Serving: Calories 332, Carbs 21g, Fat 9g, Protein 43g.

Ingredients:
- ¼ tsp black pepper
- Lemon wedges
- 4 skinless haddock fillets (6 oz.)
- ½ tsp paprika
- 1 tbsp olive oil
- ½ tsp garlic powder
- Serve with pasta, greens, rice, steamed vegetables
- 1 tsp Italian seasoning

Directions:
Put the fish on a chopping board after patting them dry with paper towels. Sprinkle the seasonings liberally on the meaty sides of the fillets after drizzling them with oil. Arrange the filets in one layer in the air fryer without crowding them. Air fry at 350 degrees F for eight to ten minutes or till thoroughly cooked and opaque. Then serve hot.

Roasted Salmon

Cooking Time: 20 min | Serves: 04 | Per Serving: Calories 348, Carbs 12g, Fat 19g, Protein 31g.

Ingredients:
- 1 ½ tsp seafood seasoning
- 10 cups baby spinach
- 1 sliced garlic clove
- 3 tsp olive oil
- ½ cup balsamic vinegar
- 4 salmon fillets (6 oz.)
- 6 small tomatoes cut into pieces
- Dash of red pepper flakes

Directions:
Preheat your air fryer to 450°F. Take a teaspoon of oil and evenly coat both sides of the salmon. Sprinkle the salmon with seafood seasoning and pepper. If necessary, cook the salmon in batches on a greased tray in the air-fryer basket. Cook until the fish starts flaking easily with a fork, which should take 10-12 mins. While the salmon is cooking, you can prepare the accompanying sauce. In a 6-quart stockpot, combine the remaining oil, garlic, and pepper flakes. Heat them over medium-low heat till the garlic becomes soft, which should take around 3-4 mins. Then, turn up the heat to medium-high and add the spinach. Cook and stir till the spinach wilts, which should take another 3-4 mins. Add the tomatoes and heat them through. Divide this mixture among 4 serving dishes. In a small saucepan, bring the vinegar to a boil. Let it simmer till the vinegar reduces by half, which should take approximately 2-3 mins. Remove it from the heat. To serve, place the cooked salmon over the bed of the spinach mixture. Finally, drizzle the balsamic glaze over the salmon, and you're ready to enjoy your meal.

Baked Crab Cakes

Cooking Time: 15 min | Serves: 03 | Per Serving: Calories 557, Carbs 56g, Fat 3g, Protein 14g.

Ingredients:
- ¾ cup panko breadcrumbs
- 2 tsp Worcestershire sauce
- 4 oz. lump crabmeat
- 3 brioche slider buns
- ½ tsp salt
- 1 egg
- ¼ tsp ground white pepper
- ¼ cup mayonnaise
- ¾ tsp Cajun seasoning
- 3 tbsp remoulade sauce

Directions:
In a mixing bowl, combine panko breadcrumbs, mayonnaise, an egg, Worcestershire sauce, Dijon mustard, Cajun seasoning, salt, cayenne pepper, and ground white pepper (if preferred). Thoroughly mix these ingredients till they form a well-combined mixture. Next, gently fold in fresh lump crabmeat, being cautious not to break up the crab too much. The aim is to keep nice, chunky pieces of crab intact. You can shape the mixture into crab cake patties of your preferred size, whether making larger ones for sandwiches or smaller ones for appetizers. Preheat your air fryer to 375°F (190°C) in bake mode. While it's heating up, prepare a parchment-lined air fryer tray or basket. Make sure not to overcrowd the tray, as you may need to bake the crab cakes in batches depending on the size of your air fryer. Place the crab cake patties onto the prepared tray or basket and bake them in the air fryer using the bake mode for approximately 10-12 mins. Remember to flip them halfway through the cooking time to ensure they're evenly golden brown and thoroughly cooked. Adjust the cooking time, if necessary, based on the size of your crab cakes. Finally, serve these delectable baked Cajun crab cakes while hot as a main dish with remoulade sauce for dipping or on brioche slider buns for some delicious sliders.

Roasted Fish Sticks

Cooking Time: 10 min | Serves: 04 | Per Serving: Calories 200, Carbs 17g, Fat 4g, Protein 26g.

Ingredients:
- ½ tsp black pepper
- ¼ cup grated parmesan cheese
- 1 tsp paprika
- ¼ cup all-purpose flour
- 1 egg
- Cooking spray
- 1 tbsp parsley flakes
- ½ cup panko breadcrumbs
- 1 lb. cod fillets

Directions:
To prepare crispy fish sticks in your air fryer, preheat it to 375°F (190°C) in roast mode. Take some cod fillets and cut them into strips to create your desired size of fish sticks. Now, set up a breading station with three shallow dishes. In the first one, place all-purpose flour. In the second, beat an egg. The third dish should contain a mixture of panko breadcrumbs, grated Parmesan cheese, parsley flakes, paprika, and black pepper. Coat each fish stick by dredging it in the flour, dipping it into the beaten egg, and generously coating it with the panko mixture, ensuring the breadcrumbs adhere well. Lay the breaded fish sticks on a parchment-lined tray or basket in your air fryer, making sure not to overcrowd them. To help them achieve that perfect crispiness, lightly spray the tops with cooking spray. Now, roast the fish sticks in the preheated air fryer for about 10-12 minutes or till they become golden brown and the fish is thoroughly cooked inside. Remember to flip them halfway through the cooking time for even browning. Once they're done, take them out of the air fryer and serve them hot. These delightful fish sticks pair wonderfully with your favorite dipping sauces, such as tartar sauce or ketchup. Enjoy your homemade crispy fish sticks!

Grilled Blackened Tilapia

Cooking Time: 08 min | Serves: 04 | Per Serving: Calories 15, Carbs 3g, Fat 0.1g, Protein 0.5g.

Ingredients:
- 1 tsp garlic powder
- 2 tbsp paprika
- 1 tsp dried oregano
- 4 tilapia fillets (6 oz.)
- ¼ tsp cayenne pepper
- 2 tsp brown sugar
- 1 tsp salt
- ½ tsp cumin

Directions:
To prepare delicious grilled, blackened tilapia in your air fryer, preheat it in grill mode, typically set to a temperature of 375°F (190°C). Mix the tilapia's blackening seasoning in a bowl by combining paprika, brown sugar, dried oregano, garlic powder, cumin, cayenne pepper, and salt. This flavorful mixture will be used to season the tilapia. Now, take the tilapia fillets and gently pat them dry with paper towels. This step is essential as it helps the seasoning adhere better and ensures even cooking. Next, evenly sprinkle the blackening seasoning onto both sides of each tilapia fillet. Use your fingers to press the seasoning onto the fillets, ensuring they are well coated. Place the seasoned tilapia fillets into the preheated air fryer's grill basket or on the grill grate if your air fryer has one. Grill the tilapia on each side for approximately 4-5 mins, or till the fish easily flakes with a fork and develops a delightful, blackened crust. Keep in mind that cooking times may vary slightly depending on the thickness of the fillets and the specific model of your air fryer, so monitor them to avoid overcooking. Once the tilapia is perfectly cooked, carefully remove it from the air fryer using tongs or a spatula. For a satisfying and flavorful meal, serve your grilled blackened tilapia piping hot, accompanied by your choice of sides such as rice, vegetables, or a fresh salad.

Grilled Mahi Mahi Tacos

Cooking Time: 15 min | Serves: 04 | Per Serving: Calories 200, Carbs 25g, Fat 8g, Protein 8g.

Ingredients:
- 1 tsp dried oregano and 1 cup sliced cabbage
- 1 tsp garlic powder and Vegetable oil
- 1 tsp dried thyme and 8 warm corn tortillas
- 1 tbsp paprika and ¼ tsp cayenne pepper
- 1 Mahi Mahi fillet(1 lb.) and 1 tsp onion powder
- Pico De Gallo & lime wedges
- 1 tsp dried thyme and ¼ cup heavy cream
- ½ tsp ground black pepper
- 2 tbsp sour cream and ¼ cup heavy cream
- 1 tsp diamond crystal kosher salt

Directions:
Begin by whisking together heavy cream, sour cream, kosher salt, black pepper, and hot sauce in a small bowl. Adjust the level of hot sauce to suit your desired level of spiciness and taste, making any necessary seasoning adjustments. Set this sauce aside for later use. For the blackening seasoning that will infuse your Mahi-Mahi with flavor, combine paprika, dried oregano, dried thyme, garlic powder, onion powder, and cayenne pepper in another small bowl. This seasoning mixture will play a key role in enhancing the taste of your fish. As you prepare to grill the Mahi-Mahi, preheat your grill to medium-high heat and lightly oil the grates to prevent sticking. Rub the Mahi-Mahi fillet with vegetable oil to ensure it doesn't adhere to the grill. Evenly sprinkle the blackening seasoning over both sides of the Mahi-Mahi fillet, pressing it onto the fish to guarantee thorough coverage. Now, it's time to grill the Mahi-Mahi. Cook it for approximately 3-4 mins on each side, or till the fish easily flakes with a fork and acquires those appealing grill marks. Once the Mahi-Mahi is perfectly grilled, remove it from the grill and allow it to rest for a few minutes. After resting, flake the fish into smaller, bite-sized pieces. To assemble your delicious grilled Mahi-Mahi tacos, warm the corn tortillas. Place a portion of the grilled Mahi-Mahi onto each tortilla, followed by thinly sliced cabbage. Finish by drizzling the creamy hot sauce over the top. For added flavor, serve these delectable tacos with pico de gallo and lime wedges on the side. Enjoy your homemade grilled Mahi-Mahi tacos!

Poultry

Bone-In Chicken Breast

Cooking Time: 25 min | Serves: 02 | Per Serving: Calories 177, Carbs 12g, Fat 6g, Protein 19g.

Ingredients:
- 1 tsp paprika
- Pinch of red paper flakes
- ½ tsp salt
- 1 tbsp oil
- ¼ cup brown sugar
- ½ tsp oregano
- 2 bone-in chicken breast
- ½ tsp garlic powder

Directions:
Preheat your air fryer to 370 degrees Fahrenheit to prepare this delicious chicken breast. While it's heating up, remove the chicken from its packaging and set it aside. Create a flavorful seasoning mixture in a bowl by combining brown sugar, paprika, garlic powder, oregano, salt, and red pepper flakes. This mixture will give your chicken a burst of flavor. Now, lightly coat both sides of the chicken with oil, ensuring they are well-covered. Then, generously coat the chicken with the brown sugar mixture, ensuring it adheres to the surface. Place the split chicken breasts into the preheated air fryer and start cooking. Cook them for approximately 25 to 30 minutes, flipping the chicken around the 10 minutes. Keep an eye on them, as thicker or larger chicken breasts may require a few extra minutes. You'll know they're done when the thickest part reaches an internal temperature of 165 degrees Fahrenheit. Once your chicken is perfectly cooked, remove it from the air fryer, and it's ready to enjoy!

Whole Chicken

Cooking Time: 55 min | Serves: 04 | Per Serving: Calories 491, Carbs 2g, Fat 22g, Protein 39g.

Ingredients:
- 1 tbsp onion powder
- 1 tbsp garlic powder
- 5 lb. whole raw chicken
- 1 tsp paprika
- 1 tbsp black pepper

Directions:
To prepare a delicious whole chicken in your air fryer, preheat it to 360 degrees. Begin by removing the neck and giblets from the chicken's cavity and patting the chicken dry with paper towels. Combine black pepper, onion powder, garlic powder, and paprika in a bowl to create a flavourful rub. Generously coat the entire chicken with this spice mixture. Place the seasoned whole chicken into the air fryer, positioning it breast side down, and cook for approximately 40 mins. After this initial cooking period, carefully flip the chicken so it is breast side up and continue cooking for 15 to 20 mins. You'll know the chicken is perfectly done when it reaches an internal temperature of 165 degrees F at its thickest point. Once your air-fried chicken is ready, remove it from the air fryer and let it rest for about 5 minutes before serving. Enjoy your succulent roasted chicken!

Orange Chicken

Cooking Time: 15 min | Serves: 02 | Per Serving: Calories 630, Carbs 46g, Fat 15g, Protein 75g.

Ingredients:
- 2 tbsp cornstarch
- 1 lb. chicken breast

Orange Sauce
- ¼ tsp ground ginger
- 2 tbsp brown sugar
- ½ cup orange juice
- 2 tsp cornstarch with 2 tsp water
- 1 tbsp rice wine vinegar
- Zest of 1 orange
- 1 tbsp soy sauce
- Dash of red pepper flakes

To serve
- Sesame seeds
- Chopped green onions

Directions:
Let's get that air fryer fired up to a sizzling 400 degrees. Here's the deal: grab your chicken pieces and toss them with some cornstarch in a bowl. Be sure not to overdo it; a light coating is all you need. It's time to air fry those coated chicken pieces. Cook them for about 7-9mins, but remember to shake that basket halfway through. We want that chicken to hit or surpass 165 degrees internally, so keep an eye on it. While the chicken's doing its thing, let's whip up that amazing orange sauce. Combine orange juice, brown sugar, rice wine vinegar, soy sauce, ginger, red pepper flakes, and a touch of orange zest in a small saucepan over a medium heat. Let that mixture come to a simmer and keep it simmering for about 5 minutes. Mix cornstarch and water in a bowl, then add it to the orange sauce. Give it a good stir and let it simmer for one more minute. Then, pull it off the heat. Once your chicken's air-fried and crispy, toss it into that luscious orange sauce. If you like, top it off with some chopped green onions and a sprinkle of sesame seeds. Now, it's time to dig in and savor every bite of this delectable dish. Enjoy!

Fried Chicken

Cooking Time: 30 min | Serves: 08 | Per Serving: Calories 558, Carbs 28g, Fat 28g, Protein 49g.

Ingredients:
- 2 tsp salt
- 2 eggs
- 3 tsp paprika
- Olive oil spray
- 2 tsp onion powder
- 3 lb. bone-in chicken thighs & drumsticks
- 2 tsp garlic powder
- 2 cups all-purpose flour
- 1 tsp black pepper
- 1 ½ cups buttermilk

Directions:
First, preheat your air fryer to a toasty 360 degrees. Take a bowl and whisk the eggs and buttermilk. Add onion powder, flour, garlic powder, pepper, paprika, and salt to another bowl. Whisk the ingredients well. Dip each piece of chicken in the flour, brushing off any excess with tongs or your hands. After that, dip it in the buttermilk and completely cover it with flour. On a baking sheet, place, and leave alone. Use the leftover chicken in the same manner. Spray the inside basket of the air fryer and the chicken pieces on all sides with olive oil spray. As many chicken pieces will fit in your air fryer basket or oven in a single layer, put 4-5 pieces on the bottom. Cook for 15 to 20 minutes. Turn the chicken over gently, then cook for 5 to 10 minutes or until the internal temperature reaches 165 degrees.

Stuffed Chicken Breast

Cooking Time: 15 min | Serves: 03 | Per Serving: Calories 524, Carbs 11g, Fat 31g, Protein 50g.

Ingredients:
- 1 ½ tsp minced garlic
- ½ cup mozzarella
- 1 ½ tsp paprika
- ¼ cup Parmesan
- 1 ½ tsp onion powder
- 2 tbsp mayo
- 4 oz. softened cream cheese
- Pepper & salt to taste
- 1 ½ tsp garlic powder
- 3 tbsp diced roasted red pepper
- ½ cup mozzarella cheese
- 3 chicken breasts (boneless & skinless)
- 1 ½ cup chopped spinach

Directions:
Firstly, season your chicken with a pinch of salt and pepper to give it that tasty kick. Now, onto the filling. In a mixing bowl, blend cream cheese, mozzarella, Parmesan cheese, mayo, minced garlic, chopped spinach, and roasted red peppers. It's going to be a creamy, cheesy, and flavorful mix. For extra flavor, we will make a seasoning mix with paprika, garlic powder, and onion powder. That's going to add a lovely kick to the dish. Take your chicken breast and carefully slice it lengthwise without going through. Lay it open like a book, and sprinkle about half to one teaspoon of the seasoning mix on one side. Then, spread roughly half a cup of that tasty spinach and cheese mixture onto one side of the chicken. Now, gently fold the chicken breast over, kind of like making a sandwich, and secure it with some toothpicks to keep all that delicious filling inside. Give the top of your chicken another sprinkle of that seasoning mix.

Here's a tip: brush olive oil in your air fryer basket instead of using nonstick spray. It'll help your basket last longer. Preheat your air fryer to 380 degrees Fahrenheit. Once it's all heated up, place two of these stuffed chicken breasts in the air fryer basket. If they won't all fit at once, no worries; cook them in batches. Let them cook for about 15 to 18 minutes or till the internal temperature reaches a safe 165 degrees Fahrenheit, as measured by a meat thermometer. Enjoy!

Cornish Hen

Cooking Time: 45 min | Serves: 02 | Per Serving: Calories 399, Carbs 1g, Fat 30g, Protein 29g.

Ingredients:
- ½ tsp black pepper
- 1 tsp paprika
- 2 tbsp olive oil
- 2 Cornish hens (1 ½ lb.)
- 2 tsp salt
- 1 tbsp lemon juice (and zest)
- 1 ½ tsp Italian seasoning
- 1 tsp garlic powder

Directions:
First off, preheat your air fryer to a cozy 360 degrees. Now, in a little bowl, whip up a flavorful mixture. Combine some oil, a pinch of salt, Italian seasoning, garlic powder, paprika, black pepper, and the zesty goodness of lemon zest and juice. This blend is going to make those hens sing with flavor. Give your Cornish game hens a gentle pat-down with a paper towel to get them nice and dry. Slather those hens with the seasoning mixture, both under and on top of the skin. Don't forget to give the wings a little twist to tuck them neatly under the birds – it's all about that perfect roast. Now, into the air fryer basket, they go, breastside down. Let them cook for about 35 minutes, and then turn the hens over. We're on a mission to get that skin all crispy and delicious, so give them an extra 10 mins. The final test: check the internal temperature. These hens are ready to shine when they hit 165 degrees Fahrenheit. Now, all that's left is to serve up those perfectly air-fried Cornish game hens and enjoy every tender, flavorful bite!

Lemon Pepper Wings

Cooking Time: 25 min | Serves: 04 | Per Serving: Calories 462, Carbs 2g, Fat 36g, Protein 31g.

Ingredients:
- 2 + 1 tsp lemon pepper seasoning
- 1 ½ lb. chicken wings
- 3 tbsp butter
- 1 tsp honey
- ½ tsp cayenne pepper

Directions:
Let's start by preheating your air fryer to a toasty 380 degrees. We're trying to make some seriously delicious lemon pepper chicken wings. Give those chicken wings a generous coating of lemon pepper seasoning and a pinch of cayenne pepper for that extra kick. We want these wings to burst with flavor! Now, into the air fryer they go, but be sure not to fill it more than halfway. We want our wings to have plenty of room to crisp up. Cook them for around 20 to 22 minutes, and don't forget to give the basket a good shake at the halfway mark. Bump the temperature to 400 degrees for 3-5 minutes to take things up a notch. That will give those wings a mouthwatering, crispy skin that's hard to resist. While those wings are sizzling away, let's whip up a tasty sauce. Mix some melted butter, a bit more lemon pepper seasoning, and some honey in a bowl. It's going to be the perfect finishing touch. Once your wings are done, pull them out of the air fryer and drizzle that lemony honey sauce all over them. Get ready to enjoy some seriously lip-smacking lemon pepper chicken wings!

Grilled Chicken

Cooking Time: 25 min | Serves: 03 | Per Serving: Calories 207, Carbs 2g, Fat 4g, Protein 38g.

Ingredients:
- 1 tsp garlic powder
- ¼ tsp cayenne pepper
- 3 chicken breast (boneless)
- ½ tsp paprika powder
- Pepper & salt to taste
- 1 tsp onion powder
- ½ tsp paprika

Directions:
First, preheat your air fryer to a nice and toasty 360 degrees. Now, let's spice things up. Mix some garlic powder, onion powder, paprika powder, cayenne powder, and a pinch of salt and pepper. This flavorful blend is going to bring those chicken breasts to life. Give those chicken breasts a good rubdown with the seasoning mix, ensuring they're coated on all sides. We want every bite to be bursting with flavor! Now, into the air fryer, they go. Cook those chicken breasts for about 20-25 minutes, but flip them over halfway through to ensure they cook evenly. Keep an eye on that internal temperature – we're looking for a safe and delicious 165 degrees. Once they're perfectly cooked, these chicken breasts are ready for action. You can enjoy them just as they are or get creative – chop them up for a salad or wrap.

Shake & Bake Chicken

Cooking Time: 20 min | Serves: 04 | Per Serving: Calories 185, Carbs 24g, Fat 4g, Protein 13g.

Ingredients:
- Water
- 4 boneless chicken breast
- 1 pack shake & bake
- 3 tbsp olive oil

Directions:
Start by preheating your air fryer to a sizzling 400 degrees Fahrenheit. Take your chicken breasts and place them on a plate. Give them a nice brush with olive oil; it'll help them get that golden, crispy coating we all love. Now, it's time to coat those chicken breasts with some Shake 'N Bake goodness. Pop open that Shake 'N Bake packet, toss it into a plastic bag that comes in the box, and give each chicken breast a good shake to coat it. Any extra coating can be discarded. Lay your beautifully coated chicken breasts in a single layer in the air fryer basket. To ensure irresistible crispiness, spray the tops of the chicken with some cooking oil spray. Let the air fryer work at 380 degrees Fahrenheit for about 14-18 minutes. Don't forget to flip those chicken breasts over once halfway through cooking. They're perfectly done when they hit an internal temperature of 165 degrees Fahrenheit. Finally, let your cooked chicken breasts rest for 5 minutes before serving them up just the way you like. Enjoy your delicious, air-fried Shake 'N Bake chicken!

Pineapple Chicken

Cooking Time: 25 min | Serves: 02 | Per Serving: Calories 503, Carbs 55g, Fat 11g, Protein 46g.

Ingredients:
- 1/8 tsp pepper
- 2 raw chicken breast
- ¼ tsp salt
- 1 tbsp butter

For Pineapple Sauce
- 2 tsp cornstarch
- ½ cup pineapple juice
- 2 tsp water
- ¼ cup brown sugar
- 1 minced garlic clove
- 1/8 tsp ground ginger
- ¼ cup soy sauce
- Fresh pineapple chunks

Directions:
Start by preheating your air fryer to a toasty 380 degrees. Combine melted butter, a pinch of salt, and some black pepper in a bowl, giving it a good mix. Coat those chicken breasts generously with this buttery goodness on both sides. Place them in the air fryer, and let them cook for 20mins, flipping them halfway through. Keep an eye on that internal temperature – we aim for a safe 165 degrees. Once they're done, let those chicken breasts rest for at least 5 mins. While your chicken is resting, let's whip up a delicious pineapple sauce. In a small saucepan over medium heat, combine pineapple juice, brown sugar, soy sauce, minced garlic, and ginger. Let that mixture simmer for about 5 minutes, allowing those flavors to meld together beautifully. Mix cornstarch and water in a separate bowl, then add it to the sauce. Keep stirring as it simmers for another minute. Then, remove it from the heat. Now, slice up those rested chicken breasts into lovely strips. You have a choice: coat the chicken entirely with that luscious sauce or pour it right over the top. For extra flavor, you can add some pineapple chunks, whether canned or fresh. And there you have it, a mouthwatering dish ready to impress! Enjoy your grilled chicken with pineapple sauce – it's a flavor explosion waiting to happen.

Chicken Tenders

Cooking Time: 12 min | Serves: 04 | Per Serving: Calories 297, Carbs 17g, Fat 13g, Protein 27g.

Ingredients:
- 1 tsp salt
- ½ cup all-purpose flour
- ¼ tsp black pepper
- 1 tsp paprika
- ½ cup buttermilk
- 1 lb. chicken tender
- ½ cup panko breadcrumbs
- ¼ tsp baking powder
- 3 tbsp melted butter
- ¼ tsp garlic powder

Directions:
Start by placing those chicken tenders into a convenient ziplock bag, pouring in the buttermilk, and squeezing out any excess air before sealing the bag. Pop this marinating wonder into the fridge and let it sit for 15-30 minutes, allowing those flavors to mingle and the tenders to soak up all that buttermilk goodness. It's time to whip up a flavorful breadcrumb coating in a shallow bowl. Combine the panko breadcrumbs, flour, baking powder, and your favorite spices. This mixture will give your chicken tenders a delightful crunch and flavor. Now, the fun part. Take those marinated chicken strips out of the buttermilk bath using a fork, allowing any extra buttermilk to drip off. Then, roll them around in the breadcrumb mixture, ensuring they're coated evenly on all sides. That's what's going to give them that irresistible crispiness. If your air fryer needs some preheating, set it to 350°F (180°C). Once ready, place your breadcrumb-coated chicken fingers into the air fryer basket. Let them air fry for around 10-12 mins, but here's the trick – pause the cooking after 4 mins to brush the chicken with melted butter. Then, flip them over and brush the other side too. Keep cooking until the internal temperature reads a safe and delicious 175°F; those tenders are golden brown and oh-so-crispy. Now, it's time to enjoy! Serve up your homemade chicken tenders with your favorite dipping sauce for a mouthwatering meal that's sure to satisfy.

Ranch Chicken

Cooking Time: 26 min | Serves: 04 | Per Serving: Calories 527, Carbs 24g, Fat 29g, Protein 39g.

Ingredients:
- ¼ cup ranch seasoning
- oil for spraying
- 1 whole chicken (broken into parts)

Directions:
You'll need a zipper bag to make these tasty ranch-seasoned chicken parts in your air fryer. Place some flour and ranch seasoning mix into that bag and give it a good shake to blend them. Now, it's time to coat your chicken parts with this flavorful seasoned flour mixture. Make sure each piece gets a nice, even coating. Once they're all coated up, place them in a single layer in your air fryer basket with the skin side down. To ensure that lovely crispiness, lightly spray them with some oil. Now, it's time to cook these beauties. Set your air fryer to 370 degrees Fahrenheit and let them cook for about 12 minutes. When that's done, give them a flip, spray lightly with oil again, and continue cooking for 12-14 mins. The goal is for the chicken to reach an internal temperature of 165 degrees, and the juices should run clear. Remember that unless you've got a large air fryer, you might need to cook this in batches. If that's the case, repeat the steps above. These cooking times are based on air fryers with a power range of 1700-1800 watts, but remember that air fryers can vary, so keep an eye on things. Now, you can enjoy some delicious ranch-seasoned chicken straight from your air fryer. Enjoy!

Turkey Breast Roast

Cooking Time: 50 min | Serves: 06 | Per Serving: Calories 348, Carbs 12g, Fat 5g, Protein 59g.

Ingredients:
- 1/3 cup brown sugar
- 1 pinch salt
- 2 cups water
- Black pepper as per taste
- 1/3 cup kosher salt
- 1 frozen turkey breast roast (3 lb.)
- 2 tbsp butter

Directions:
First, thaw the frozen turkey breast in the refrigerator for about 24 hours. Next, create a flavorful brine by boiling water and stirring in kosher salt, brown sugar, and pepper. Let the brine cool completely for about 30 mins. Place the turkey breast in a container and cover it with the cooled brine, adding more water to ensure the turkey is fully submerged. Let it brine for 8 hours or overnight in the refrigerator. Once the turkey has brined, preheat your air fryer to 390°F (200°C) according to the manufacturer's instructions. Remove the turkey from the brine, dry it, and rub it with butter. Season it generously with seasoned salt and pepper. Now, it's time to air-fry the turkey. Cook it for 15 minutes, then turn it, remove any netting, and season it again. Reduce the temperature to 360°F (182°C), continue cooking for 20 minutes, and turn it again after 15 minutes. Finally, increase the temperature to 390°F (200°C), turn the turkey once more, and cook until it's no longer pink in the center, which usually takes 15 more mins. Once the turkey is perfectly cooked, remove it from the air fryer and let it rest for about 5 minutes before slicing and serving. Enjoy your air-fried turkey breast!

Chicken Skewers

Cooking Time: 20 min | Serves: 07 | Per Serving: Calories 130, Carbs 8g, Fat 4g, Protein 15g.

Ingredients:
- 1 tsp chili powder
- 1 yellow, green, and red bell pepper, each cut into inches
- 1 tsp garlic powder
- 1 zucchini cut into pieces
- Cooking spray
- 1 tbsp avocado oil
- 1 tsp ground ginger
- 1 red onion cut into pieces
- 1 tbsp honey
- 16 oz. boneless & skinless chicken breast (cut into pieces)
- 1 tbsp low-sodium tamari (soy sauce)

Directions:
For this delicious chicken and veggie skewer recipe, start by marinating the chicken. Place the chicken in a bowl and drizzle it with oil. Mix soy sauce, garlic, ginger, chili powder, and honey in a separate bowl to create a flavorful sauce. Pour this sauce over the chicken and toss everything together. Let the chicken marinate for at least 15 minutes or overnight for more flavor. Next, it's time for assembly. Lay out your veggies, and then start threading the chicken and veggies onto skewers. Alternate between chicken and veggies, layering them until the skewers are nicely filled, leaving about ½ inch on each end for easy handling. Now, onto cooking. Preheat your air fryer to 350 degrees Fahrenheit. Place a skewer holder inside the air fryer basket and arrange the chicken and veggie skewers on top. Give them a quick spray with cooking spray. Cook for 7-9 mins, turning the skewers over halfway through the cooking time. To ensure the chicken is perfectly cooked, ensure it reaches an internal temperature of 165 degrees. Depending on the size of your air fryer, you might need to cook these in batches. Finally, serve your flavorful skewers over rice or with your favorite sides, whether it's potatoes, a green salad, or pasta salad. Enjoy your tasty and easy air-fried skewers!

Chicken Nuggets

Cooking Time: 15 min | Serves: 20 | Per Serving: Calories 341, Carbs 16g, Fat 25g, Protein 30g.

Ingredients:
- ¾ cup Italian breadcrumbs
- ½ tsp Italian seasoning
- Pepper & salt
- ½ tsp garlic powder
- 1 chicken breast cut into chunks
- ½ cup melted butter

Directions:
For these tasty chicken nuggets, start by trimming excess fat from your chicken breast and cutting it into bite-sized chunks. Season the chicken with salt and pepper, and let it come to room temperature. Mix breadcrumbs, garlic powder, and Italian seasoning in a separate bowl. In another bowl, melt some butter. Dip each chicken nugget in the melted butter first, then coat it with the breadcrumb mixture. Preheat your air fryer to 390°F. Place the nuggets in the basket; spraying it is unnecessary since the chicken is coated with butter. Cook for 10-12 mins, flipping them halfway through. Keep an eye on them towards the end, as cooking times may vary depending on your air fryer. Once they're golden and crispy, your chicken nuggets are ready to enjoy!

Sesame Chicken Thighs

Cooking Time: 15 min | Serves: 04 | Per Serving: Calories 485, Carbs 7g, Fat 33g, Protein 40g.

Ingredients:
- 2 tbsp toasted sesame seeds
- 1 tbsp honey
- 1 tsp rice vinegar
- 2 tbsp sesame oil
- 1 chopped green onion
- 1 tbsp sriracha sauce
- 2 lb. chicken thighs
- 2 tbsp soy sauce

Directions:
To prepare this delicious dish, combine sesame oil, soy sauce, honey, sriracha, and rice vinegar in a large bowl. Add the chicken to the mixture and give it a good stir. Cover the bowl and let the chicken marinate in the refrigerator for at least 30 minutes. Next, preheat your air fryer to 400°F (200°C). Drain the marinade from the chicken. Place the chicken thighs in the air fryer basket, skin-side up. Cook for 5 mins, flip them, and continue cooking for 10 minutes. Once they're done, transfer the chicken to a plate and let it rest for about 5 minutes before serving. To add some extra flavor, garnish with green onions and sesame seeds. Enjoy your scrumptious air-fried chicken!

Chicken Calzone

Cooking Time: 15 min | Serves: 02 | Per Serving: Calories 397, Carbs 50g, Fat 21g, Protein 12g.

Ingredients:
- 1/3 cup shredded chicken breast
- Cooking spray
- 1/3 cup shredded mozzarella cheese
- 1 tsp olive oil
- 3 cups baby spinach leaves
- 6 oz. prepared pizza dough
- 1/3 cup low sodium marinara sauce
- ¼ cup chopped red onion

Directions:
Start by heating some oil in a nonstick skillet over medium-high heat. Add diced onions and sauté until they become tender, which takes about 2 mins. Next, stir in fresh spinach, cover the skillet, and let it cook until the spinach wilts, which typically takes around 1.5 mins. Once done, remove it from the heat and mix in marinara sauce and cooked chicken. Now, let's get your air fryer ready. Preheat it to 325°F (165°C) following the manufacturer's instructions. Take your pizza dough and divide it into four equal portions. Roll each piece on a lightly floured surface into a 6-inch circle. Spread a quarter of the spinach mixture on the bottom half of each dough circle. Top it with a quarter of the mozzarella cheese. Fold the dough over the filling to create a half-moon shape, then crimp the edges to seal it shut. Coat the calzones generously with cooking spray. Transfer your calzones to the air fryer basket. Cook them for about 8 minutes. Afterward, flip the calzones over and cook until they turn a lovely golden brown, usually taking about 4 minutes more. Your delicious calzones are now ready to enjoy!

Chicken Cutlet

Cooking Time: 20 min | Serves: 01 | Per Serving: Calories 333, Carbs 20g, Fat 08g, Protein 41g.

Ingredients:
- 2 tbsp grated parmesan cheese
- 1 tsp all-purpose flour
- 3 tbsp seasoned breadcrumbs
- Cooking spray
- Dash of onion, garlic powder & pepper
- 2 tbsp buttermilk
- 1 lb. chicken breast half (6 oz.)

Directions:
Follow these simple steps for a delightful chicken dish in your air fryer. Mix flour, garlic powder, onion powder, and pepper in a shallow bowl. In another bowl, combine cheese and buttermilk. Place breadcrumbs in a third shallow bowl. Preheat your air fryer to 400°F. Take your chicken and gently flatten it to about 1/4-inch thickness. Now, coat the chicken by dipping it in the flour, buttermilk, and breadcrumbs. Place the coated chicken on a greased tray in the air fryer basket and give it a spritz with cooking spray. Cook until it turns a beautiful golden brown and is no longer pink inside, typically around 20-25 mins. Don't forget to flip it over once during cooking for even browning. Now, you're ready to savor your crispy and delicious air-fried chicken!

Chicken Taco Pockets

Cooking Time: 25 min | Serves: 08 | Per Serving: Calories 393, Carbs 29g, Fat 24g, Protein 16g.

Ingredients:
- ½ cup sour cream
- 2 tbsp taco seasoning
- 1 cup shredded cheddar cheese
- 2 tubes crescent rolls (8 oz. each)
- ½ cup salsa
- Guacamole, shredded lettuce, and sour cream (optional)
- 1 cup shredded rotisserie chicken

Directions:
Start by preheating your air fryer to 375°F. Now, unroll one tube of crescent dough and divide it into 2 rectangles, sealing the perforations. Repeat the same with the second tube of dough. Mix salsa, sour cream, and taco seasoning in a bowl. Spoon chicken on the left side of each dough rectangle and top it with the salsa mixture. Sprinkle with cheese, then fold the dough over the filling, sealing the edges by pinching them. Work in batches to place these pockets on the tray in your air fryer basket if needed. Cook until they turn a lovely golden brown, usually taking about 20-25 mins. Once they're done, cut these delicious pockets in half and serve them with salsa and your preferred toppings. Enjoy your air-fried chicken pockets!

Chicken Meatballs

Cooking Time: 10 min | Serves: 12 | Per Serving: Calories 98, Carbs 9g, Fat 3g, Protein 9g.

Ingredients:
- ½ tsp garlic powder
- 2 tbsp lime juice
- ½ tsp salt
- 2 tbsp ketchup
- 1 tsp soy sauce
- 1 tbsp minced cilantro
- ¾ cup panko breadcrumbs
- 1 beaten egg
- ½ cup sweet chili sauce
- 1 chopped green onion
- 1lb. Lean ground chicken

Directions:
To make these flavorful chicken meatballs in your air fryer, preheat it to 350°F. In a small bowl, combine chili sauce, lime juice, ketchup, and soy sauce, setting aside 1/2 cup of this mixture for later. Mix an egg, bread crumbs, green onion, cilantro, salt, garlic powder, and the remaining 4 tablespoons of the chili sauce mixture in a larger bowl. Then, add the chicken and gently combine everything, forming 12 meatballs. In batches, arrange these meatballs in a single layer on a greased tray in your air fryer basket. Cook until they're lightly browned, typically taking about 4-5 mins. Flip them over and continue cooking until they're browned and cooked through another 4-5 mins. Once done, serve these tasty chicken meatballs with the reserved sauce, and you can sprinkle some extra cilantro on top for added flavor. Enjoy your delicious air-fried chicken meatballs!

Meat

Pork Belly Bites

Cooking Time: 25 min | Serves: 04 | Per Serving: Calories 177, Carbs 12g, Fat 6g, Protein 19g.

Ingredients:
- 1 tbsp brown sugar
- 1 tsp kosher salt
- 3 tbsp canola oil
- 1 tsp garlic powder
- 1 ½ lb. pork belly cut into pieces
- 1 tsp pepper

Directions:
Start by preheating your air fryer to a toasty 400°F. In a good-sized bowl, create a flavor-packed mixture by combining oil, brown sugar, garlic powder, salt, and a dash of pepper. Give it all a good stir to make sure those flavors meld together beautifully. It's time to introduce your pork belly pieces to this delicious concoction. Ensure each piece gets coated nicely with the oil mixture; we want them to be thoroughly dressed for the occasion. Lay those flavorful pork belly pieces in a single layer within the basket of your air fryer. Depending on the size of your air fryer, you might need to do this in two or three batches. The goal is to make sure they have enough room to cook evenly. Let's get these pork belly cubes air frying! Cook them for about 18-20 minutes, but remember to give the basket a good shake and flip those cubes a few times during cooking. Remember that the exact cooking time can vary based on the size of your pork belly pieces and the capacity of your air fryer. Once perfectly cooked, remove those delicious pork belly cubes from the air fryer, ready to be savored. Serve them up while they're warm, and enjoy the incredible flavors!

Pork Roast

Cooking Time: 50 min | Serves: 06 | Per Serving: Calories 461, Carbs 30g, Fat 35g, Protein 35g.

Ingredients:
- 2 tsp kosher salt
- 1 tbsp olive oil
- 2 lb. pork roast (boneless pork loin roast)

Directions:
First, get your pork roast ready by patting it dry. If it happens to have a rind, take a sharp knife and score the skin in a criss-cross pattern, making sure to cut into the fat beneath, but not into the meat itself. Now, it's time to give that pork roast some flavor. Sprinkle some salt generously over the skin and rub it in. Let it sit for about 10 minutes to allow the salt to work its magic by drawing out moisture from the skin. After the wait, pat the pork roast dry once more, and then drizzle it with a bit of oil, giving it a good rub to ensure the flavors coat the meat evenly. Preheat your air fryer oven to a perfect 360°F (180°C). Once it's nice and hot, place your prepared pork roast in the air fryer basket. Now, let it cook for about 50 minutes, with a general guideline of 25 minutes of cooking time for each pound of meat. When the cooking time is up, it's essential to check that the pork is cooked to perfection. Ensure it has reached an internal temperature of 145°F (63°C) right at the center of the thickest part. Here's a pro tip: remove the pork roast from the air fryer, cover it with some kitchen foil, and let it rest for a blissful ten minutes before slicing it into delectable slices to serve. Enjoy your tender and flavorful air-fried pork roast!

Pork Chops

Cooking Time: 20 min | Serves: 02 | Per Serving: Calories 230, Carbs 16g, Fat 6g, Protein 25g.

Ingredients:
- ¼ tsp salt
- 2 trimmed boneless pork chops (5 oz.)
- ¼ tsp onion powder
- ½ cup panko breadcrumbs
- ¼ tsp garlic powder
- Cooking spray
- 1 tsp paprika

Directions:
Here's what you need to do to create a delicious crispy pork dish in your air fryer. Start by combining panko breadcrumbs, paprika, garlic powder, and onion powder in a large zip-top plastic bag. Once they're all in there, add the pork, seal the bag, and shake it well until it is nicely coated with the breading mixture. Take the pork out of the bag and shake off any excess breading. Place these nicely coated pork pieces into the air fryer basket, and to ensure that perfect crispiness, give them a light coating of cooking spray. Set your air fryer to 360°F and let the magic happen. Cook the pork until it's beautifully browned and the internal temperature, checked with an instant-read thermometer inserted into the thickest part, reaches a safe 145°F. This usually takes about 15 to 17 mins. Once your air-fried pork is perfectly cooked, transfer it to a plate and let it rest for a relaxing 5 mins. Just before serving, sprinkle some salt evenly over the top. Now, your crispy, flavorful pork is ready to enjoy!

Lamb Roast

Cooking Time: 15 min | Serves: 02 | Per Serving: Calories 181, Carbs 12g, Fat 11g, Protein 18g.

Ingredients:
- ½ tsp black pepper
- 1 tbsp olive oil
- 1 tsp rosemary
- 10 oz. boneless butter-filled lamb leg roast
- 1 tsp thyme

Directions:
Creating a delectable lamb roast using your air fryer is a breeze. Preheat your air fryer to a delightful 360°F (180°C). Now, let's infuse some flavors into that lamb roast. Mix olive oil, rosemary, and thyme on a plate. Take your lamb roast, pat it well to ensure it's dry, and then place it into this herb and oil mixture, ensuring it gets a nice coating. Once your lamb is well-coated, it's time to place it in the air fryer basket. Set your air fryer to 360°F (180°C) and let it cook for about 15-20 mins. This should result in a medium-cooked lamb, but it's always a good idea to check the temperature with a meat thermometer to ensure it's cooked to your liking. If you prefer it to be more well-done, you can cook it in additional 3-minute intervals. When your air-fried lamb roast is perfectly cooked, remove it from the air fryer and cover it with kitchen foil. Allow it to rest for about five minutes; this resting period lets the juices reabsorb into the meat, ensuring it's tender and succulent. Finally, carve the lamb roast against the grain for the perfect presentation and flavor. Your air-fried lamb roast is now ready to be savored!

Lamb Chops

Cooking Time: 08 min | Serves: 04 | Per Serving: Calories 350, Carbs 10g, Fat 19g, Protein 42g.

Ingredients:
- ½ tsp kosher salt
- 1 tbsp red wine vinegar
- ½ tsp garlic powder
- 1/4 tsp black pepper
- 2 tbsp olive oil
- 1 tsp dried rosemary
- ½ tsp oregano
- 1.5 lb. lamb chops

Directions:
Start by combining your lamb chops with olive oil, red wine vinegar, rosemary, oregano, salt, garlic powder, and black pepper in a bowl. Rub this flavorful marinade into the meat, ensuring each chop gets a generous coating. Cover the bowl and let it chill in the refrigerator for a relaxing hour, allowing those flavors to meld. Now, it's time to fire up your air fryer. Preheat it to a sizzling 400 degrees Fahrenheit, getting it nice and hot for cooking. Add marinated lamb chops to the basket once your air fryer is ready. Let them cook for about 7-9 minutes, but don't forget to give them a flip halfway through the cooking process. This ensures that both sides get that perfect golden sear. When your air-fried lamb chops are cooked to your preferred level of doneness, they're ready to be savored. The marinated flavors will be infused into the meat, making every bite a delight. Enjoy your perfectly cooked lamb chops straight from the air fryer!

Country Style Ribs

Cooking Time: 20 min | Serves: 04 | Per Serving: Calories 627, Carbs 4g, Fat 42g, Protein 60g.

Ingredients:
- Barbecue sauce
- 2 lb. country style pork ribs
- Head country seasoning

Directions:
To prepare these delicious air-fried ribs, start by preheating your air fryer to 375°F, allowing it to get nice and hot for about 5 mins. In the meantime, take your ribs and generously coat them with your preferred seasoning and sauce, ensuring they are well-covered for that perfect flavor. Now, it's time to prepare the air fryer basket for cooking. Give it a light spray with the cooking oil or spray you choose to prevent sticking. This step will help you achieve that crispy exterior while keeping the meat tender on the inside. Once your air fryer is heated and the ribs are seasoned and sauced, carefully place the ribs into the prepped air fryer basket. Set the temperature to 375°F and let them cook for 20 minutes. Remember to flip the ribs after the first 10 minutes to ensure even cooking and a beautifully caramelized exterior. As the ribs cook, monitor their internal temperature. You'll want them to reach at least 145°F for safe consumption, but you can adjust the cooking time according to your preference for doneness. Whether you like them tender and falling off the bone or with a bit more bite, the air fryer method makes it easy to achieve that mouthwatering, savory goodness. Enjoy your homemade air-fried ribs!

Beef Roast

Cooking Time: 60 min | Serves: 06 | Per Serving: Calories 620, Carbs 3g, Fat 43g, Protein 56g.

Ingredients:
- 1 pack gravy mix
- 4 tbsp unsalted butter
- 1 tsp steak seasoning
- ½ cup water
- 3 lb. beef chuck roast
- Rosemary or parsley to garnish

Directions:
Begin by preheating your air fryer to 390°F for approximately 5 mins. While the air fryer is heating up, season your roast evenly with your favorite steak seasoning, ensuring a flavorful coating. Next, create the gravy mixture by combining your brown gravy with 1/2 cup of water and set it aside for later use. Once the preheating is complete, lightly spray the inside of the air fryer with your chosen cooking oil spray, such as grapeseed oil, to prevent sticking. Now, carefully place the seasoned roast into the preheated air fryer. Let it cook at 390°F for 15 minutes to achieve a beautiful sear on the outside, sealing in those savory juices. After this initial searing step, prepare a sheet of aluminum foil to place the roast on. Gently remove the roast from the air fryer and position it on the foil. Roll the foil around the roast, ensuring the sides are open to allow air circulation. With the roast securely wrapped in foil, it's time to add the flavorful elements. Pour the brown gravy mixture evenly over the roast and place a generous pat of butter on top. Lower the air fryer temperature to 325°F and continue cooking for 30-40 mins. Keep a close eye on the roast's internal temperature; it should reach at least 145°F for safe consumption. Once your roast reaches the desired doneness, carefully remove it from the air fryer. Allow it to rest for 5 minutes before slicing and serving. Don't forget to serve the roast with its delicious drippings as a delectable gravy. Enjoy your homemade air-fried roast!

Beef Tips

Cooking Time: 10 min | Serves: 04 | Per Serving: Calories 307, Carbs 07g, Fat 16g, Protein 31g.

Ingredients:
- 2 tbsp brown sugar
- 1 tbsp crushed garlic
- Grapeseed oil spray
- 1 tbsp grated ginger
- 2 tbsp gluten-free soy sauce
- 1 lb. boneless beef sirloin steak (cut into chunks)
- ½ tbsp Worcestershire sauce

Directions:
To create this tasty dish, start by preparing the marinade. Combine the soy sauce, Worcestershire sauce, brown sugar, ginger, and garlic in a small bowl. Mix these ingredients well to form a flavorful marinade. Grab a large Ziploc bag and pour the prepared marinade into it. Place the cut sirloin steak into the bag, ensuring it's completely coated with the marinade. Seal the bag securely, and it's a good idea to put it inside another pan or container in case of leaks. Place this marinating steak in the refrigerator for a recommended marinating time of 2 hours, allowing those delicious flavors to infuse the meat. Once the sirloin steak has fully marinated, it's time to get your air fryer ready for action. Coat the bottom of the air fryer basket with grapeseed oil spray to prevent sticking. Carefully arrange the marinated beef evenly in the air fryer basket. Then, set the air fryer temperature to 390°F and cook for 8-10 mins, depending on your preferred level of doneness. This cooking method ensures a quick and flavorful result. To complete your meal, serve the air-fried sirloin steak with your choice of sides. Popular options include broccoli or noodles but feel free to get creative with your favorite accompaniments. Enjoy your homemade air-fried steak dish!

Steak Wrapped Asparagus

Cooking Time: 10 min | Serves: 06 | Per Serving: Calories 432, Carbs 07g, Fat 29g, Protein 43g.

Ingredients:
- 4 tbsp balsamic vinegar
- 1 crushed garlic clove
- 2 cups halved grape tomatoes
- 1 tsp salt
- 1 ½ lb. thinly sliced skirt steak
- Olive oil cooking spray
- 1 lb. trimmed asparagus
- 4 tbsp olive oil

Directions:
To prepare this delectable dish, lightly spray the basket with olive oil spray, ensuring the ingredients won't stick during cooking. Now, slice your steak into 6 even pieces, cutting against the grain for the best texture. In a small bowl, combine vinegar, oil, garlic, and salt, giving it a light mix. It's okay if the mixture doesn't fully combine; you want the flavors to meld. Next, assemble the steak and asparagus rolls. Take about 3 asparagus spears and place them on one slice of steak, then roll it up and secure it. Continue this process until you've prepared all the steak and asparagus rolls. Depending on the size of your basket, you may be able to fit 3 at a time. Add half of the tomatoes to the mix once you have 3 rolls in the basket.

Using a brush, generously coat the steak and vegetables with the oil and vinegar. It's time to cook these savory rolls using the air crisp function. Set the temperature to 390 degrees and cook for approximately 10 minutes using the attached lid. However, checking on them at the 5-minute mark is good, as cooking preferences can vary. You'll want to ensure they reach your desired level of doneness. Carefully remove the first batch and repeat the process for the remaining 3 steak and asparagus rolls. To serve, plate the steak-wrapped asparagus with the tomatoes. This dish combines the rich flavors of steak with the freshness of asparagus and tomatoes for a delightful culinary experience. Enjoy!

Cheeseburger Pockets

Cooking Time: 10 min | Serves: 04 | Per Serving: Calories 382, Carbs 07g, Fat 24g, Protein 33g.

Ingredients:
- Sharp shredded cheddar cheese
- 1 lb. cooked & drained ground beef
- 1 can of biscuits (8 count)

Directions:
Follow these straightforward steps to create these tasty stuffed biscuit pockets using your air fryer. Begin by taking the biscuits from the can and gently flattening each one, either by hand or with a rolling pin, until they form thin circles. On four flattened biscuits, evenly distribute portions of ground beef and top them with shredded cheddar cheese, ensuring a generous layer of cheese. Then, select another biscuit from the can, leaving it without any toppings, and place it on top of one of the beef and cheese-covered biscuits. Stretch the dough gently to encase the filling completely and form a pocket. Seal the edges using a fork to ensure the contents are securely enclosed. To prepare your air fryer for cooking, grease the basket to prevent sticking. Depending on the size of your air fryer, you may be able to fit two pockets at a time. If desired, give the pockets a light coating of olive oil cooking spray to help achieve a beautiful golden-brown finish. Set your air fryer to 360°F and cook the pockets for 4-5 mins, but remember that cooking times can vary between air fryers, so it's wise to check their progress around the 3–4-min mark. Once they are nicely browned, your biscuit pockets will be ready to enjoy.

Nachos

Cooking Time: 05 min | Serves: 06 | Per Serving: Calories 597, Carbs 54g, Fat 35g, Protein 20g.

Ingredients:
- 1 ½ cups cooked ground beef chili
- 4 cups tortilla chips
- 2 cups shredded cheese

Directions:
Begin by filling the air fryer basket up to about one-third of its capacity with tortilla chips. Next, layer on approximately half of your prepared ground beef chili and sprinkle it generously with cheese. Now, add another layer of tortilla chips, filling the basket to about two-thirds full, and top this layer with the remaining portion of your cooked chili and more cheese. With your nachos beautifully assembled in the air fryer basket, it's time to cook them perfectly. Set the air fryer temperature to 350°F (180°C) and cook for approximately 3-5 mins, or until the cheese has melted and the nachos are nicely heated. Once they're done, carefully remove your mouthwatering nachos from the air fryer, and they're ready to serve. This quick and easy recipe ensures you'll have a crowd-pleasing snack or appetizer in no time. Enjoy your homemade air-fried nachos!

Taco Pie

Cooking Time: 26 min | Serves: 04 | Per Serving: Calories 403, Carbs 28g, Fat 22g, Protein 25g.

Ingredients:
- ½ cup diced tomatoes
- 1 cup shredded cheddar cheese
- 1 tbsp oil
- ½ cup Bisquick
- 1 cup diced onion
- 2 eggs
- ½ cup corn kernels
- 1 cup chopped lettuce
- 8 oz. ground beef
- 1 cup milk
- 1 tbsp taco seasoning

Directions:
Heat oil in a skillet over medium heat to prepare this delicious dish. Saute the chopped onion for about 3 minutes until it becomes translucent and slightly softened. Then, introduce your choice of protein, cooking it until it's thoroughly done. Once your protein is cooked, incorporate the spices and corn into the skillet, stirring everything together to ensure the flavors meld. Whisk together Bisquick, milk, and eggs in a separate small bowl until they form a smooth mixture. Add this mixture to the skillet, combining it with the other ingredients in the pan. Now, transfer the entire skillet mixture into the oiled air fryer pot. Set your air fryer to 370°F (190°C) and cook for 16 mins. Be sure to stir it at the 10-minute mark to ensure even cooking. After the initial 14 minutes of cooking, sprinkle some cheese over the top and continue air frying for another 2 minutes until the cheese is nicely melted and bubbly. To serve, top your savory creation with diced tomatoes and fresh lettuce.

Beef and Bean Taquitos

Cooking Time: 10 min | Serves: 20 | Per Serving: Calories 181, Carbs 14g, Fat 09g, Protein 11g.

Ingredients:
- 1 pack of taco seasoning
- 1 cup shredded cheddar cheese
- 20 white corn tortillas
- 1 lb. ground beef
- 1 can of refried beans

Directions:
To prepare these delicious air-fried beef and bean burritos, cook the ground beef if it isn't already cooked. Brown the meat over medium-high heat and follow the taco seasoning instructions on the package to season it to your liking. It's time to prepare the corn tortillas with the seasoned beef ready. Warm them up in the microwave for about 20 seconds to make them pliable. This step is essential for corn tortillas to prevent tearing when rolled. To prevent sticking, either spray the air fryer basket with non-stick cooking spray or line it with a sheet of foil and spray. Now, assemble your burritos. Place a portion of the seasoned ground beef, beans, and a sprinkle of cheese onto each tortilla. Roll them up tightly, ensuring the seams are on the bottom, to keep the fillings secure. Before air frying, give the burritos a quick spray of cooking oil, such as olive oil spray. Set your air fryer to 390 degrees and cook the burritos for 5 mins. After that time, carefully flip them over and cook for 2-3 minutes or until they're nicely browned on top. Repeat these steps for any additional tortillas you'd like to make.

Meatballs

Cooking Time: 10 min | Serves: 06 | Per Serving: Calories 417, Carbs 22g, Fat 22g, Protein 30g.

Ingredients:
- 1 tsp minced garlic
- ¼ cup grated Parmesan cheese
- 1 tsp onion powder
- ¾ cup Italian-style breadcrumbs
- 1 tsp salt
- 1 tbsp dried parsley flakes
- ¼ tsp ground black pepper
- 1 ½ lb. ground beef
- 1 beaten egg

Directions:
To prepare these flavorful meatballs using your air fryer, begin by taking a large mixing bowl. Combine the ground beef, breadcrumbs, chopped parsley, minced garlic, diced onion, egg, grated Parmesan cheese, salt, and pepper in this bowl. Gently mix all these ingredients until combined, being careful not to overmix. It's time to shape the meat mixture into meatballs, approximately 1 inch in size. Place these meatballs into the air fryer basket, ensuring they're not touching each other to allow for proper air circulation. Depending on the size of your air fryer basket, you may need to cook them in batches. Set your air fryer to 400 degrees Fahrenheit (200 degrees Celsius) and cook the meatballs for about 10 minutes or until they reach an internal temperature of 165 degrees Fahrenheit (74 degrees Celsius). Once they're cooked to perfection, carefully remove the meatballs from the air fryer and keep them warm. You can repeat the process with the remaining meat mixture to cook the rest of the meatballs.

Beef & Bean Chimichangas

Cooking Time: 08 min | Serves: 10 | Per Serving: Calories 580, Carbs 66g, Fat 22g, Protein 29g.

Ingredients:
- ½ cup Colby jack cheese (shredded)
- 1 lb. ground beef
- ½ cup refried beans
- 10 flour tortillas (taco size)
- 1 pack of taco seasoning
- Toppings of your choice

Directions:
To prepare these delicious chimichangas using your air fryer, start by browning the ground beef in a skillet. Add the taco seasoning according to the package instructions as the meat cooks to infuse it with flavor. Mix in the refried beans once the ground beef is cooked and seasoned to create a savory filling. Now, it's time to assemble the chimichangas. Place a portion of the beef and bean mixture in the center of each tortilla and top it with a generous amount of shredded cheese. Fold the tortilla over the filling to ensure that all the delicious ingredients are securely tucked inside. To prevent sticking, spray your air fryer basket with non-stick cooking spray or olive oil spray. Carefully place the chimichangas seam side down in the air fryer basket, ensuring they're not too crowded. You can also give them a light spray with olive oil or avocado cooking spray for a crisp finish. Set the air fryer temperature to 360 degrees Fahrenheit and cook the chimichangas for approximately 8 mins. Check on them at the 5-minute mark to ensure they are cooking nicely. Once done, the chimichangas should have a lightly browned appearance on top, and the tortilla will be nicely secured around the flavorful filling.

Manwich Sloppy Joe Bombs

Cooking Time: 25 min | Serves: 16 | Per Serving: Calories 118, Carbs 02g, Fat 07g, Protein 10g.

Ingredients:
- 1 cup mozzarella cheese
- A can of Manwich
- 1 egg
- 1 lb. ground beef
- 1 can flakey biscuit

Directions:
To prepare these savory Manwich sloppy joe bombs, start by browning ground beef in a medium-sized skillet. Once cooked, drain the excess fat and then mix in the can of Manwich sauce. Allow the meat to cool completely. This recipe is convenient for leftovers, too. Flatten your biscuit dough either by hand or with a rolling pin. In the center of each dough round, add approximately 2 tablespoons of shredded cheese. Then, spoon about 1/4 cup of the cooled meat mixture on the mozzarella. To seal these delicious bombs, gently pinch the sides of the dough together. Afterward, roll the filled dough in the palm of your hand to form a neat ball, and place it on a tray or in the basket of your air fryer, which you've sprayed with non-stick cooking spray. For a golden finish, brush the tops of the dough balls with an egg wash. It's time to cook these delectable creations in your preheated air fryer. Set the temperature to 375°F and cook for 8 minutes. Afterward, flip them over and cook for an additional 8 minutes. For the final step, flip them and cook for about 4 more minutes until they become golden brown and are no longer doughy inside. Once done, allow the Manwich sloppy joe bombs to sit and cool for about 5 minutes before serving.

Pizza Burgers

Cooking Time: 15 min | Serves: 04 | Per Serving: Calories 534, Carbs 32g, Fat 28g, Protein 43g.

Ingredients:
- 1 tbsp tomato paste
- ½ tsp salt
- 6 oz. mozzarella cheese
- 1 tsp Italian seasoning
- Freshly ground black pepper
- 1 cup pizza sauce
- 1 lb. meatloaf mix of ground pork, veal & beef
- 1/3 cup chopped pepperoni
- 4 round rolls (ciabatta or focaccia bread)
- 1 tbsp minced onion

Directions:
To whip up these delectable pizza burgers, combine the meatloaf mixture, minced onion, pepperoni, tomato paste, Italian seasoning, salt, and pepper in a large bowl. Thoroughly mix everything until it's well combined. Divide the meat into four equal portions and shape them into hamburger patties, being careful not to over-handle the meat. A handy trick is tossing the meat between your hands gently compacting it each time. Flatten the patties, creating a slight indentation in the center of each one to help them cook evenly. Next, take your rolls and split them in half, brushing the cut side with a touch of olive oil. Preheat your air fryer to 370°F. Place the burger patties in the preheated air fryer and cook for 15 minutes, flipping them halfway through the cooking time. During the last few minutes of cooking, spoon some pizza sauce onto each burger and top them with sliced mozzarella cheese. Continue air frying at 370°F for 3 minutes or until the cheese has melted to perfection. Once done, carefully remove the burger patties from the air fryer and let them rest. Now, place the cut side of the rolls into the air fryer and air fry at 380°F for 2 to 3 mins to achieve a delightful toasting. Finally, transfer the rested burgers onto the toasted rolls, sprinkle more Italian seasoning on top for that extra flavor, and serve these pizza burgers immediately. This mouthwatering dish combines the best of pizza and burgers for a satisfying meal. Enjoy!

Taco Pizza

Cooking Time: 08 min | Serves: 04 | Per Serving: Calories 611, Carbs 29g, Fat 35g, Protein 44g.

Ingredients:
- 1 ½ cups shredded lettuce
- 1 pack of taco seasoning
- Black olives
- 4 pizza dough
- 1 ½ cups shredded Mexican-style cheese
- 15 oz. drained ranch-style beans
- Catalina dressing
- 1 lb. ground beef
- Fritos

Directions:
To make these delicious pan-style pizzas in the air fryer, begin by browning the ground beef and following the taco seasoning instructions indicated on the package. Once the beef is seasoned to perfection, set it aside. Now, grab one pizza crust and begin assembling your first pizza. Layer the seasoned ground beef, beans, and a generous amount of shredded cheese onto the pizza crust. Carefully place this pizza into the basket of your air fryer and set the temperature to 375°F. Cook for about 8 minutes until it reaches a delightful golden-brown finish. When it's done, take the pizza out and add your preferred additional toppings. Finish it by drizzling Catalina Dressing over the pizza to enhance its flavor. Repeat these steps for each additional pizza. This recipe allows you to create four individual pan-pizza-sized pizzas in total.

Spiral Ham

Cooking Time: 30 min | Serves: 20 | Per Serving: Calories 300, Carbs 16g, Fat 25g, Protein 30g.

Ingredients:
- Glaze
- 1 pre-cooked & completely thawed spiral ham

Directions:
To make delicious air-fried ham, preheat your air fryer to 300°F (149°C). If your ham is too large to fit into the air fryer, you can cut it off the bone to make it fit. Place the ham into the air fryer basket and air fry it for 15 minutes at 300°F (149°C). While the ham is cooking, prepare the glaze. After the initial 15 minutes, flip the ham upside down and generously apply the glaze all over its surface. Cook the ham for 15 minutes at 300°F (149°C). To ensure the ham is thoroughly cooked, use a meat thermometer to check that it has reached an internal temperature of at least 145°F (63°C). If the ham needs more time, add extra cooking time as needed. Once the ham is perfect, serve it with your choice of sides, such as mashed potatoes, carrots, or any other accompaniments you prefer. Enjoy your air-fried ham!

Bacon-Wrapped Hot Dogs

Cooking Time: 15 min | Serves: 08 | Per Serving: Calories 203, Carbs 9g, Fat 15g, Protein 8g.

Ingredients:
- 8 strips bacon
- 8 hot dogs

Directions:
To prepare these bacon-wrapped hot dogs, wrap each hot dog with your desired amount of bacon, as per your preference (note that bacon strips can vary in size). Next, place up to 4 hot dogs at a time on the steamer rack, positioned in the lowest position or the air fryer basket. Ensure you adequately space the hot dogs for proper air circulation during cooking. Now, set your air fryer to a temperature of 360 degrees Fahrenheit (182 degrees Celsius) and cook for 15 mins. After this cooking time, check the hot dogs for your desired level of doneness. If they need more time or the bacon isn't cooked to your liking, you can continue cooking them in additional 1-2 min increments until both the hot dogs and bacon are cooked to your desired perfection. These bacon-wrapped hot dogs make for a savory and satisfying treat, perfect for enjoying on various occasions.

Vegetables

Stuffed Sweet Potatoes

Cooking Time: 50 min | Serves: 02 | Per Serving: Calories 376, Carbs 28g, Fat 25g, Protein 12g.

Ingredients:
- ¼ tsp kosher salt
- 1 cup shredded cheddar cheese
- ¼ tsp pepper
- 1 chopped green onion
- 2 tbsp butter
- 2 crumbled cooked bacon strips
- 1/3 cup toasted chopped pecans
- 1 tsp olive oil
- ¼ cup chopped cranberries
- 2 sweet potatoes
- 1 cup cooked spinach (chopped)

Directions:
To prepare these scrumptious stuffed potatoes in your air fryer, preheat it to 400°F (204°C). Give your potatoes a gentle brush with some oil to help achieve a crispy texture. Place them on the tray inside your air fryer basket and cook until tender, typically 30-40 mins. Once done, allow the potatoes to cool slightly. Now, it's time to transform these potatoes into flavorful stuffed delights. Cut each potato in half lengthwise and carefully scoop out the pulp, leaving a 1/4-inch thick shell. Transfer the potato pulp to a large bowl. In the same bowl, mash the potato pulp, then fold in the spinach, 3/4 cup of cheese, bacon, diced onion, dried cranberries, chopped pecans, butter, salt, and pepper. Ensure everything is thoroughly mixed. Spoon this delightful mixture back into the potato shells, mounding it slightly to fill them up nicely. Reduce the air fryer's temperature to 360°F (182°C), place the stuffed potato halves in the basket, and cut side up. Let them cook for 10 more minutes at this slightly lower temperature. After this time, sprinkle the remaining 1/4 cup of cheese over the top and continue cooking until the cheese has melted, which usually takes 1-2 mins. Once the cheese is perfectly melted, your mouthwatering stuffed potatoes are ready to be savored. Whether served as a delightful side dish or a satisfying main course, these air-fried stuffed potatoes will surely be a hit. Enjoy!

Garlic-Herb Fried Patty Pan Squash

Cooking Time: 25 min | Serves: 04 | Per Serving: Calories 58, Carbs 6g, Fat 3g, Protein 2g.

Ingredients:
- ¼ tsp pepper
- 2 minced garlic cloves
- ¼ tsp dried thyme
- 1 tbsp olive oil
- ½ tsp salt
- 1 tbsp minced parsley
- ¼ tsp dried oregano
- 5 cups halved patty pan squash (1 ½ lb.)

Directions:
To prepare this delicious air-fried squash dish, preheat your air fryer to 375°F. While it's heating up, place your squash in a spacious bowl. Combine the oil, minced garlic, salt, oregano, thyme, and pepper in a separate container to create a flavorful drizzle. Once the mixture is well combined, generously drizzle it over the squash in the bowl, ensuring it is evenly coated. Give it a gentle toss to make sure every piece is nicely covered. It's time to transfer the seasoned squash onto a greased tray in the air fryer basket. Cook the squash until it becomes tender, usually 10-15 mins. Don't forget to stir the squash occasionally during the cooking process to ensure even cooking and a wonderful golden finish. Once the squash reaches the desired level of tenderness, please remove it from the air fryer and sprinkle it with freshly chopped parsley. This adds a burst of color and an extra layer of flavor to the dish.

Beets with Orange Gremolata and Goat Cheese

Cooking Time: 25 min | Serves: 12 | Per Serving: Calories 49, Carbs 9g, Fat 1g, Protein 2g.

Ingredients:
- 2 tbsp lime juice
- 1 tsp grated orange zest
- 2 tbsp orange juice
- ½ tsp salt
- 1 tbsp minced parsley
- 1 lb. fresh beets
- 3 tbsp crumbled goat cheese
- 1 lb. golden beets
- 2 tbsp sunflower kernel
- 1 tbsp minced sage

Directions:
To create this flavorful beet dish using your air fryer, preheat it to 400°F. Start by giving the beets a good scrub and trimming the tops to leave about 1 inch. Place the prepared beets on a double layer of heavy-duty foil, roughly 24x12 inches. Fold the foil around the beets, sealing it tightly to create a packet. Now, arrange this packet in a single layer on the tray within the air fryer basket. Allow the beets to cook in the air fryer until they become tender, typically taking 45-55 mins. When done, carefully open the foil packet to let the steam escape. Once the beets are cool enough to handle, peel, halve, and slice them, placing them in a serving bowl. In a separate container, combine lime juice, orange juice, and salt, and then toss this mixture with the beets to coat them evenly. Mix parsley, sage, garlic, and orange zest to add flavor, and then sprinkle this aromatic blend over the beets. Top it off with crumbled goat cheese and sunflower kernels for an extra texture and taste. You can serve this delightful beet dish, either warm or chilled, making it a versatile and delicious addition to your meal. Enjoy!

Bacon Wrapped Avocado Wedges

Cooking Time: 30 min | Serves: 12 | Per Serving: Calories 142, Carbs 3g, Fat 13g, Protein 3g.

Ingredients:
- 2 tbsp lime juice
- 12 bacon strips
- ½ cup mayonnaise
- 1 tsp grated lime zest
- 2 ripe avocados
- 3 tbsp sriracha chili sauce

Directions:
To prepare these delectable bacon-wrapped avocado wedges using your air fryer, preheat it to 400°F. Start by slicing each avocado in half, carefully removing the pit, and then peeling them. Take each avocado half and cut it into thirds, resulting in wedges. It's time to wrap each avocado wedge with a slice of bacon, ensuring it securely encircles the avocado. You may need to work in batches to accommodate all the wedges. Place them in a single layer on the tray within the air fryer basket. Cook the bacon-wrapped avocado wedges in the air fryer until the bacon is cooked, which typically takes 10-15 mins. While the wedges are cooking, you can prepare a delightful dipping sauce. In a small bowl, stir mayonnaise, Sriracha sauce, lime juice, and zest. This sauce adds a zesty kick to complement the savory bacon-wrapped avocados. Once the wedges are done cooking, serve them alongside the spicy mayo dipping sauce. These air-fried bacon-wrapped avocado wedges make for a mouthwatering appetizer or snack, perfect for any occasion. Enjoy!

Roasted Green Beans

Cooking Time: 20 min | Serves: 06 | Per Serving: Calories 76, Carbs 8g, Fat 5g, Protein 3g.

Ingredients:
- ¼ tsp salt
- 1 sliced red onion
- 1/8 tsp pepper
- 2 tbsp olive oil
- 1 lb. green beans cut into small pieces
- 1 tsp Italian seasoning
- ½ lb. sliced mushrooms

Directions:
To make these delightful air-fried vegetables, preheat your air fryer to 375°F. In a spacious bowl, combine all the ingredients and give them a good toss to ensure they are evenly coated with the seasonings. Next, arrange the seasoned vegetables on a greased tray within the air fryer basket. Cook them until they reach a state of tenderness, which should take about 8-10 mins. Then, give the veggies a toss to redistribute them, and then continue cooking until they achieve a beautiful, golden-brown appearance. This second cooking phase also typically takes 8-10 minutes. Your air-fried vegetables can be a delicious side dish or a healthy snack. This method provides a convenient and flavorful way to prepare your favorite veggies. Enjoy!

Mushroom Roll-Ups

Cooking Time: 30 min | Serves: 10 | Per Serving: Calories 291, Carbs 31g, Fat 16g, Protein 8g.

Ingredients:
- 8 oz. finely chopped portobello mushrooms
- 1 tsp dried thyme
- Cooking spray
- 1 tsp dried oregano
- 10 flour tortillas
- 8 oz. softened cream cheese
- ½ tsp crushed red pepper flakes
- Chutney
- ¼ tsp salt
- 2 tbsp olive oil
- 4 oz. ricotta cheese

Directions:
To prepare these delectable mushroom and cheese roll-ups using your air fryer, heat some oil in a skillet over medium heat. Add the mushrooms to the skillet and sauté them for about 4 minutes until they soften. Add in the oregano, thyme, red pepper flakes, and salt, and continue to sauté the mushrooms until they turn beautifully browned, typically taking 4-6 more mins. Once done, set this mushroom mixture aside to cool. Combine the cheeses in a separate bowl, then gently fold in the sautéed mushrooms, ensuring they are well incorporated into the cheese mixture. Now, it's time to assemble the roll-ups. Spread approximately 3 tablespoons of the mushroom and cheese mixture onto the bottom center of each tortilla. Roll up the tortillas tightly and secure them with toothpicks. Preheat your air fryer to 400°F. Place the roll-ups in batches on a greased tray within the air-fryer basket and give them a quick spritz with cooking spray. Cook the roll-ups until they turn a lovely golden brown, which should take about 9-11 mins. Once the roll-ups are done and cooled enough to handle, remove the toothpicks. These flavorful mushroom and cheese roll-ups are best served with chutney.

Eggplant Parm

Cooking Time: 10 min | Serves: 04 | Per Serving: Calories 173, Carbs 22g, Fat 6g, Protein 9g.

Ingredients:
- ½ cup marinara sauce
- 1 egg
- ½ tsp garlic powder
- ¼ cup grated parmesan cheese
- 1 eggplant
- ¼ cup Italian breadcrumbs
- ½ tsp dried basil
- ½ cup shredded mozzarella cheese

Directions:
Cut the eggplant into about 1/4 inch thick slices to prepare this delicious air-fried eggplant parm. Place these eggplant slices in a colander or on a baking sheet and generously sprinkle them with salt. Allow the salted eggplant to sit for a minimum of 15 minutes; this helps draw out excess moisture. Meanwhile, preheat your air fryer to 370 degrees Fahrenheit. To coat the eggplant, set up two bowls: one with beaten egg and the other with a mixture of breadcrumbs, Parmesan cheese, garlic powder, and basil. First, dip each eggplant slice into the beaten egg, ensuring it's well coated. Then, coat the eggplant slice in the breadcrumb mixture, fully covering each slice. Now, carefully arrange each breaded eggplant slice in a single layer in your air fryer basket, ensuring they are not touching. Cook the slices for about 8 to 10 minutes, flipping them halfway through the cooking time. You can spritz the slices with some oil for a crispier texture during this process. Once the eggplant slices are nicely air-fried and have a golden hue, it's time to add the toppings. Place a teaspoon of marinara sauce on each eggplant slice, followed by a generous sprinkle of mozzarella cheese. Close the air fryer and continue to cook for an additional 1 min. Afterward, turn off the air fryer and let the eggplant parm sit for one more minute to allow the cheese to melt fully. Finally, carefully remove the eggplant parm from the air fryer and savor the delightful flavors. This air-fried eggplant parm is a delicious and healthier twist on a classic dish. Enjoy!

Eggplant Fries

Cooking Time: 08 min | Serves: 04 | Per Serving: Calories 278, Carbs 34g, Fat 11g, Protein 12g.

Ingredients:
- 1 tsp garlic powder
- 2 eggs
- 1 cup panko breadcrumbs
- Oil spray
- ½ cup grated parmesan
- 1 eggplant sliced into sticks

Directions:
Preheat your air fryer to 400 degrees Fahrenheit to make these delicious air-fried eggplant fries. Next, take the eggplant and cut it into stick-shaped pieces. There's no need to remove the skin of the eggplant for this recipe. Combine the panko breadcrumbs, Parmesan cheese, and garlic powder in a bowl. This mixture will provide a crispy and flavorful coating for the eggplant fries. In a separate bowl, whisk together the eggs to create an egg wash. Now, dip each eggplant stick into the egg wash, ensuring it's thoroughly coated, and then transfer it to the bowl with the panko mixture. Press the stick into the panko mixture on all sides to ensure it's evenly covered. Place the coated eggplant fries into the air fryer basket, arranging them in a single layer. To enhance their crispiness, give the tops of the fries a light spray with an oil. Cook the eggplant fries in the air fryer for approximately 7 to 8 minutes, flipping them halfway through the cooking time for even browning and crispiness. Once golden brown and crispy, your eggplant fries are ready to be served. They make for a delicious snack or appetizer, especially when paired with marinara sauce or your favorite dipping sauce. Enjoy!

Broccoli & Cauliflower

Cooking Time: 10 min | Serves: 04 | Per Serving: Calories 124, Carbs 13g, Fat 8g, Protein 5g.

Ingredients:
- ½ tsp garlic powder
- 2 tbsp olive oil
- 1 tsp Italian seasoning
- 3 cups broccoli florets
- ½ tsp salt
- 3 cups cauliflower florets

Directions:
To prepare this delightful air-fried broccoli and cauliflower, preheat your air fryer to 375°F. Next, take the broccoli and cauliflower florets and toss them in a bowl with olive oil, Italian seasoning, garlic powder, and a pinch of salt. Make sure the vegetables are evenly coated with this flavorful mixture. Once your vegetables are seasoned to perfection, add them to the air fryer basket. Cook them for about 10 minutes, remembering to shake the basket gently once at the halfway point of the cooking time. This ensures that the broccoli and cauliflower cook evenly and develop a lovely texture and flavor. After the cooking, your air-fried broccoli and cauliflower are ready to be served as a delicious and healthy side dish. Enjoy!

Bok Choy

Cooking Time: 04 min | Serves: 06 | Per Serving: Calories 30, Carbs 3g, Fat 2g, Protein 2g.

Ingredients:
- ½ tsp garlic powder
- Pepper & salt to taste
- 1 tbsp sesame seeds
- 4 baby bok choy
- ½ tsp sesame oil

Directions:
To prepare this flavorful air-fried bok choy, preheat your air fryer to 370 degrees Fahrenheit. Begin by washing the bok choy thoroughly and then slicing it in half. Take a medium-sized glass bowl and place the bok choy halves in it. Add the sesame seeds, sesame oil, and garlic powder to the bowl, and toss everything together to ensure the bok choy is evenly coated with these delightful flavors. Now, transfer the seasoned bok choy to the basket of your preheated air fryer. Cook the bok choy at 370 degrees F for approximately 6 mins, remembering to stir or flip the bok choy halfway through the cooking time. This step ensures the bok choy cooks evenly and becomes tender with a hint of crispiness. Once the bok choy is perfectly cooked, remove it from the air fryer, and it's ready to be enjoyed as a delicious and nutritious side dish. Savor the wonderful flavors of this air-fried bok choy!

Desserts

Air Fried Oreos

Cooking Time: 05 min | Serves: 08 | Per Serving: Calories 172, Carbs 32g, Fat 4g, Protein 2g.

Ingredients:
- 1 pack of crescent rolls
- 8 oreo cookies
- Powdered sugar

Directions:
To make these delightful Air Fryer Oreos, spread the crescent dough onto a cutting board or countertop. Use your finger to press down on each perforated line, essentially forming one large sheet of dough. Then, cut the dough into eighths. Now, place an Oreo cookie in the center of each crescent roll square. Carefully roll up each corner of the dough to envelop the Oreo, ensuring it's fully covered. Be cautious not to stretch the crescent roll too thinly, as this could cause it to break. Preheat your air fryer to 320 degrees Fahrenheit for 2-3 mins. Gently place the Air Fryer Oreos inside the air fryer in a single row, ensuring they do not touch. If your air fryer is smaller, you may need to cook them in batches. Cook the Oreos at 320 degrees for approximately 5-6 minutes till they achieve a golden-brown exterior. Once they are done, carefully remove the Air Fryer Oreos from the air fryer. If desired, dust them with powdered sugar immediately. Allow the Air Fryer Oreos to cool for about two minutes, and then they're ready to be enjoyed as a delicious treat. Indulge in the warm, crispy goodness of these delightful treats!

S'MORES

Cooking Time: 04 min | Serves: 04 | Per Serving: Calories 216, Carbs 32g, Fat 9g, Protein 3g.

Ingredients:
- 4 graham cracker sheet
- 12 squares from a chocolate bar
- 4 marshmallows

Directions:
Preheat your air fryer to 380 degrees Fahrenheit to create these delectable air-fried s' mores. Start by placing graham crackers in the air fryer basket and generously topping them with marshmallows. You can also use a wire rack to keep the marshmallows from flying around. Cook these delightful treats for about 3 to 4 minutes or until the marshmallows turn a golden brown that suits your taste. Carefully remove the s'mores from the air fryer once the marshmallows have achieved that perfect golden hue. Now, it's time to elevate these s'mores to the next level of deliciousness. Add three squares of chocolate to each s'more, and then complete the sandwich with the other graham cracker. Your air-fried s'mores are ready to be savored. Delight in the gooey marshmallows, creamy chocolate, and crispy graham crackers that make up this classic treat. Enjoy!

Cookies

Cooking Time: 08 min | Serves: 18 | Per Serving: Calories 161, Carbs 21g, Fat 8g, Protein 2g.

Ingredients:
- 1/3 cup granulated sugar
- 1 tsp baking soda
- 1/3 cup brown sugar
- ½ tsp salt
- ½ cup softened butter
- 1 tsp vanilla extract
- 1 ½ cup flour
- 1 egg
- 1 cup chocolate chips

Directions:
To whip up these delicious chocolate chip cookies in your air fryer, mix the butter and sugars in a mixing bowl until the mixture becomes light and fluffy. Then, add the egg and vanilla extract and beat the mixture until well combined. Sift the flour, baking powder, and salt in a separate bowl. Once sifted, add this dry mixture to the butter mixture and mix thoroughly until all the ingredients are well incorporated. Don't forget to toss in those chocolate chips and give it a good stir. Preheat your air fryer to 300 degrees Fahrenheit and line the basket with air fryer parchment paper that has holes to allow for proper air circulation. Now, it's time to shape the cookie dough. Form small golf ball-sized portions of dough and gently flatten each one slightly. Place these cookie dough rounds into the air fryer basket. Cook the cookies in the air fryer for approximately 6-8 minutes or until they turn a beautiful golden brown on top. After cooking, allow the cookies to rest in the basket for at least 5 minutes before carefully removing them to cool on a wire rack. These delightful air-fried chocolate chip cookies will satisfy your sweet tooth with soft centers and slightly crisp edges. Enjoy your homemade treats!

Lava Cake

Cooking Time: 10 min | Serves: 02 | Per Serving: Calories 776, Carbs 77g, Fat 51g, Protein 10g.

Ingredients:
- 1 tbsp powdered sugar
- ¼ tsp salt
- 4 tbsp butter
- ½ cup powdered sugar
- 2 tbsp Nutella
- ½ cup semi-sweet chocolate chips
- 1 tbsp softened butter
- 2 eggs
- 1 tsp vanilla extract
- 3 tbsp all-purpose flour

Directions:
To create these delectable chocolate lava cakes using your air fryer, preheat it to 370 degrees Fahrenheit. In a medium microwave-safe bowl, combine the chocolate chips and butter. Heat this mixture in the microwave in 30-second intervals until it's completely melted and smooth, stirring between intervals to ensure even melting. Add the eggs, vanilla extract, a pinch of salt, flour, and ½ cup powdered sugar to this smooth chocolate mixture. Whisk everything together until well combined. In a separate bowl, prepare the Nutella filling by mixing Nutella, softened butter, and 1 tbsp powdered sugar until it forms a smooth and creamy mixture. Now, it's time to prepare the ramekins. Spray them with a bit of oil to prevent sticking. Fill each ramekin halfway with the chocolate chip mixture.

Add a generous dollop of the Nutella filling into the center of each ramekin. Cover the Nutella with the remaining chocolate chip mixture, ensuring it's completely concealed. Carefully place these filled ramekins into your preheated air fryer and cook for approximately 8 to 11 minutes. Keep an eye on them to ensure they cook to your desired level of gooeyness. Once done, carefully remove the lava cakes from the air fryer and allow them to cool for about 5 minutes. Use a butter knife to run around the cakes' edges gently, then flip them onto serving plates. To finish, top your chocolate lava cakes with a scoop of ice cream, a drizzle of chocolate syrup, or other favorite toppings.

Peach Cobbler

Cooking Time: 10 min | Serves: 02 | Per Serving: Calories 105, Carbs 24g, Fat 1g, Protein 2g.

Ingredients:
- ½ tsp cinnamon
- 1 cup peach slices
- 1 tsp cornstarch
- 1/3 cup milk
- 2 tbsp sugar
- ½ cup Bisquick

Directions:
Start by preheating the air fryer at 360 Degrees Fahrenheit. Take two one-cup ramekins and grease them. Add sugar, half of the cinnamon, peach slices, and cornstarch in a bowl. Mix all the ingredients till they are coated well on peach slices. Divide the slices into greased ramekins. Take another bowl and mix milk, bisquick, and remaining cinnamon. Dived this mixture into the two ramekins. Place the ramekins inside the air fryer and cook for 10 mins or till the top is golden brown and everything is thoroughly cooked. Let peach cobbler sit for five mins then serve it with chilled ice cream.

Cinnamon Sugar Dessert Fries

Cooking Time: 15 min | Serves: 04 | Per Serving: Calories 110, Carbs 18g, Fat 4g, Protein 1g.

Ingredients:
- ½ tsp cinnamon
- 1 tbsp melted butter
- 2 sweet potatoes
- 1 tsp melted butter
- 2 tbsp sugar

Directions:
To prepare these scrumptious sweet potato fries in your air fryer, preheat it to 380 degrees Fahrenheit. Begin by peeling the sweet potatoes and cutting them into thin, fry-like strips. Take the cut sweet potato fries and coat them with 1 tablespoon of butter, ensuring they're nicely covered. Now, arrange the coated fries in the preheated air fryer. They can overlap, but ensure they don't fill the air fryer more than halfway to allow proper air circulation. Let the sweet potato fries cook in the air fryer for approximately 15-18 mins. They should become golden and crispy during this time. Once they're done, carefully remove the sweet potato fries from the air fryer and transfer them to a bowl. Add the remaining butter to the bowl and sprinkle the sugar and cinnamon. Give everything a good mix to coat the fries evenly with this delightful blend of flavors. Now, your mouthwatering sweet potato fries are ready to be enjoyed immediately. Savor the sweet and cinnamon-kissed goodness of this tasty snack!

Pumpkin Pie Twists

Cooking Time: 06 min | Serves: 08 | Per Serving: Calories 219, Carbs 25g, Fat 13g, Protein 2g.

Ingredients:
- ½ cup confectionery sugar
- 2 & ¼ tsp milk
- 2 tbsp melted unsalted butter
- 1 can of crescent rolls
- 2 tsp pumpkin pie spice
- 1/8 tsp salt
- 2 tbsp melted butter
- ½ cup pumpkin puree

Directions:
To whip up these delightful Air Fryer Pumpkin Pie Twists, begin by rolling out the crescent roll dough and pressing it down to smooth out any perforated lines. You can cut the dough into eighths to create smaller twists for smaller air fryers, but quarters will work for most. Mix the pumpkin puree, half of the pumpkin pie spice, and a pinch of salt until well combined. Spread this pumpkin mixture evenly on top of the crescent roll dough. Then, layer two of the crescent dough sheets on top of the other two, ensuring that the corners and sides align as closely as possible. Now, use a dough or pizza cutter to slice each pumpkin twist sheet into four long strips, giving you eight twists. Preheat your air fryer to 320 degrees Fahrenheit for 2-3 minutes to prepare it for action. Take each strip and give it a twist at the bottom and then again at the top to create that signature twist shape.

To add a touch of buttery goodness, brush melted butter on top of the pumpkin pie twists and sprinkle them with the remaining pumpkin pie spice. Place these delectable twists into the air fryer in a single layer, ensuring they don't touch. Let them cook for about 6 minutes. While the twists are air frying, prepare the icing by whisking together confectionery sugar, melted butter, and milk in a separate bowl. Once the Air Fryer Pumpkin Pie Twists are done, remove them and drizzle them with the prepared icing. You can savor these delightful treats immediately or store them in the refrigerator for up to 3 days. Enjoy the sweet and spicy pumpkin goodness!

Brownies

Cooking Time: 20 min | Serves: 06 | Per Serving: Calories 341, Carbs 47g, Fat 15g, Protein 05g.

Ingredients:
- ¼ cup brown sugar
- ½ tsp vanilla
- 1/5 cup chocolate chips
- 4 tbsp salted butter
- ¼ cup cocoa powder
- 1 egg
- ¼ cup white sugar
- ¼ cup plain flour
- ¼ cup milk chocolate chunks

Directions:
To create this delectable brownie treat, prepare two mini loaf pans or one regular-sized loaf pan by lining them with baking paper. Begin by placing the butter, brown sugar, white sugar, and cocoa powder in a microwave-safe bowl. Microwave this mixture in 20-second increments, stirring it well after each interval, until the butter is melted and everything is well combined. Once achieved, add the vanilla and stir it in. Allow the bowl to sit for a moment to cool slightly. Next, mix in the egg, then incorporate the flour until thoroughly combined. Fold in the chocolate chips, and if you desire an extra burst of chocolatey goodness, add the optional chocolate chunks. Now, evenly distribute the batter among the prepared mini loaf pans. If you use a single regular-sized loaf pan, pour the batter into it. Pop your brownie creation into the air fryer, preheated to 160°C (320°F). Bake it for around 20-25 mins, or until a toothpick inserted into the center comes out with just a few fudgy crumbs clinging to it. Allow the brownie to rest in the loaf pans for about 10 minutes to cool slightly, then carefully transfer it to a wire rack to cool completely. Once cooled, you're ready to savor this delightful homemade treat!

Apple Hand Pies

Cooking Time: 15 min | Serves: 08 | Per Serving: Calories 220, Carbs 25g, Fat 12g, Protein 3g.

Ingredients:
- 1 egg
- 2 pie crusts (pre-made)
- 5 oz. can of apple pie filling

Directions:
To create these delightful apple hand pies, roll out the pie crust and use a cookie cutter to create circular shapes. Now, take a small amount, about half a spoonful, of apple pie filling and position it in the center of half of your circular crusts. For the remaining crust circles, gently roll them out with a rolling pin so they're slightly larger than the ones with apple filling. Place the larger circles atop the apple-filled ones, and use a fork to seal the edges together firmly. Give each apple hand pie a light egg wash to give it a lovely golden finish. Now, it's time to cook these beauties in your air fryer. Set the temperature to 350 degrees Fahrenheit and cook the hand pies for approximately 12-15 mins. Once they're done, serve and relish these scrumptious homemade apple hand pies. Enjoy!

Bread Pudding

Cooking Time: 15 min | Serves: 06 | Per Serving: Calories 375, Carbs 53g, Fat 14g, Protein 9g.

Ingredients:
- ¼ cup chocolate chips
- ½ tsp vanilla extract
- 2/3 cup heavy cream
- 1 egg
- ¼ cup sugar
- 2 cups cubed bread

Directions:
To prepare this delicious bread pudding in your air fryer, begin by greasing the inside of a baking dish that fits snugly inside the air fryer. Next, place the bread cubes into the greased baking dish. If you're adding chocolate chips for an extra treat, sprinkle them evenly over the bread. In a separate bowl, combine the egg, whipped cream, vanilla, and sugar to create a creamy mixture. Pour this delightful egg mixture over the bread cubes in the baking dish and allow it to soak for about 5 minutes. Now, carefully place the baking dish into the air fryer basket. Set the air fryer temperature to 350°F and cook the bread pudding for approximately 15 minutes or until it's perfectly cooked. Once done, savor your homemade bread pudding's warm and comforting flavors. Enjoy!

Conclusion

As we close with the Vortex Dual Basket Air Fryer Oven Cookbook, we hope this culinary adventure has been entertaining and educational. This cookbook aims to arm you with the information and meal ideas you need to get the most out of your Vortex Dual Basket Air Fryer. We've looked at various recipes throughout the cookbook, including breakfasts, lunches, appetizers, side dishes, fish, poultry, meat, vegetables, and desserts. You may experiment with different cooking methods and flavors thanks to the versatility and convenience of your air fryer oven, which we've highlighted with each dish. The appliance provides a useful way to prepare healthier meals without compromising taste in a time-constrained society. We hope the tips and recipes in this book have encouraged you to be more inventive in the kitchen while streamlining your culinary techniques. So may your future culinary explorations with the Vortex Dual Basket Air Fryer Oven be filled with robust flavors, delightful textures, and truly rewarding cooking. Enjoy creating wonderful meals in your dependable air fryer oven, and here's to many more!

Conversion Charts

Mass

Imperial (ounces)	Metric (gram)
¼ ounce	7 grams
½ ounce	14 grams
1 ounce	28 grams
2 ounces	56 grams
3 ounces	85 grams
4 ounces	113 grams
5 ounces	141 grams
6 ounces	150 grams
7 ounces	198 grams
8 ounces	226 grams
9 ounces	255 grams
10 ounces	283 grams
11 ounces	311 grams
12 ounces	340 grams
13 ounces	368 grams
14 ounces	396 grams
15 ounces	425 grams
16 ounces/ 1 pound	455 grams

Cups & Spoon

Cups	Metric
¼ cup	60 milliliters
1/3 cup	80 milliliters
½ cup	120 milliliters
1 cup	240 milliliters

Spoon	Metric
¼ teaspoon	1¼ milliliters
½ teaspoon	2½ milliliters
1 teaspoon	5 milliliters
2 teaspoons	10 milliliters
1 tablespoon	20 milliliters

Liquid

Imperial	Metric
1 fluid ounce	30 milliliters
2 fluid ounces	60 milliliters
3½ fluid ounces	80 milliliters
2¾ fluid ounces	100 milliliters
4 fluid ounces	125 milliliters
5 fluid ounces	150 milliliters
6 fluid ounces	180 milliliters
7 fluid ounces	200 milliliters
8¾ fluid ounces	250 milliliters
10½ fluid ounces	310 milliliters
13 fluid ounces	375 milliliters
15 fluid ounces	430 milliliters
16 fluid ounces	475 milliliters
17 fluid ounces	500 milliliters
21½ fluid ounces	625 milliliters
26 fluid ounces	750 milliliters
35 fluid ounces	1 Liter
44 fluid ounces	1¼ Liters
52 fluid ounces	1½ Liters
70 fluid ounces	2 Liters
88 fluid ounces	2½ Liters

Temperature

Fahrenheit (°F)	Celsius (°C)
275°F	140°C
300°F	150°C
325°F	165°C
350°F	177°C
375°F	190°C
400°F	200°C
425°F	220°C
450°F	230°C
450°F	230°C
475°F	245°C
500°F	260°C

Notes

Printed in Great Britain
by Amazon